Letters of Tribulation

Jorge Mario Bergoglio, SJ
POPE FRANCIS

Letters of Tribulation

Edited by Antonio Spadaro, SJ, and Diego Fares, SJ

Maryknoll, New York 10545

Founded in 1970, Orbis Books endeavors to publish works that enlighten the mind, nourish the spirit, and challenge the conscience. The publishing arm of the Maryknoll Fathers and Brothers, Orbis seeks to explore the global dimensions of the Christian faith and mission, to invite dialogue with diverse cultures and religious traditions, and to serve the cause of reconciliation and peace. The books published reflect the views of their authors and do not represent the official position of the Maryknoll Society. To learn more about Maryknoll and Orbis Books, please visit our website at www.orbisbooks.com.

Copyright © 2018, La Civiltà Cattolica, Rome
Copyright © 2018, Libreria Editrice Vaticana, Vatican City

English edition, copyright © 2020 by Orbis Books

The permissions listed on page 161 of this book represent an extension of this copyright page.

Published by Orbis Books, Box 302, Maryknoll, NY 10545-0302.

All rights reserved.

No part of this publication may be reproduced or transmitted in any form or by any means, electronic or mechanical, including photocopying, recording, or any information storage or retrieval system, without prior permission in writing from the publisher.

Queries regarding rights and permissions should be addressed to: Orbis Books, P.O. Box 302, Maryknoll, NY 10545-0302.

Manufactured in the United States of America

Library of Congress Cataloging-in-Publication Data

Names: Francis, Pope, 1936– author. | Spadaro, Antonio, editor. | Fares, Diego, 1955– editor.
Title: Letters of tribulation / Jorge Mario Bergoglio, S.J., POPE FRANCIS ; edited by Antonio Spadaro, S.J. and Diego Fares, S.J.
Other titles: Correspondence. English
Description: English edition. | Maryknoll, NY : Orbis Books, 2020. | Some letters written previously to being Pope. | Summary: Pope Francis draws on wisdom from Superiors General of the Jesuit order in the past to confront painful ordeals in the church today.
Identifiers: LCCN 2020006720 (print) | LCCN 2020006721 (ebook) | ISBN 9781626983915 (paperback) | ISBN 9781608338559 (ebook)
Subjects: LCSH: Catholic Church—History—1965– | Consolation. | Francis, Pope, 1936—correspondence.
Classification: LCC BX1390 .F6813 2020 (print) | LCC BX1390 (ebook) | DDC 282.09/051—dc23
LC record available at https://lccn.loc.gov/2020006720
LC ebook record available at https://lccn.loc.gov/2020006721

Contents

Preface
   Pope Francis   vii

Introduction
   Antonio Spadaro, SJ   ix

PART ONE
The Tribulations of Yesterday

The Doctrine of Tribulation
   Jorge Mario Bergoglio, SJ   3

LETTERS OF THE SUPERIORS GENERAL OF THE SOCIETY OF JESUS TO THE FATHERS AND BROTHERS OF THE SOCIETY

LETTER OF LORENZO RICCI, SJ (September 26, 1758)	13
LETTER OF LORENZO RICCI, SJ (December 8, 1759)	16
LETTER OF LORENZO RICCI, SJ (November 30, 1761)	22
LETTER OF LORENZO RICCI, SJ (November 13, 1763)	30
LETTER OF LORENZO RICCI, SJ (January 16, 1765)	42
LETTER OF LORENZO RICCI, SJ (June 17, 1769)	45

CONTENTS

Letter of Lorenzo Ricci, SJ (February 22, 1773)   50

Letter of Jan Roothaan, SJ (July 24, 1831)   56

Against the Spirit of Fury
   Diego Fares, SJ   67

PART TWO
The Tribulations of Today

Pope Francis
"The open, painful, and complex wound of sex abuse"
FOUR LETTERS TO THE CHURCH OF CHILE

Guide to Reading the Letters to the Church of Chile
   Diego Fares, SJ   91

   Letter to the Bishops of Chile (April 8, 2018)   109

   Letter to the Bishops of Chile (May 15, 2018)   113

   Letter to the Bishops of Chile (May 17, 2018)   128

   Letter to the Pilgrim People of God
      in Chile (May 31, 2018)   129

Pope Francis
"Eradicating the Culture of Abuse"
LETTER TO THE PEOPLE OF GOD

Guide to Reading the Letter to the People of God
   James Hanvey, SJ   143

   Letter to the People of God (August 20, 2018)   153

Preface

Pope Francis

I remember when I offered Father Miguel Ángel Fiorito, SJ, the draft of the preface I had written for the first edition of the *Letters of Tribulation*. The Master (we called him that because that is what he was, and what he remains today, given his accomplishment in forming a school of discernment) asked me to further develop the last paragraph, where I had mentioned the importance of having recourse to self-reproach (cf. *Spiritual Exercises*, 48).

That section had to do with discerning and dealing with the external shame and confusion that reign when the Evil One unleashes a fierce persecution against the children of the Church by confronting that persecution with the healthy shame and confusion with which the infinite Mercy of the Lord and his Faithfulness provide those who seek forgiveness for their sins. "There is a grace there," he told me. "Develop that."

Thirty years later we are in a different context, yet the War is the same, and it is the Lord's. These *Letters* are "a treatise on discernment in times of confusion and tribulation." Their re-publication finds us still besieged, yet determined, together with our colleagues who have shared their reflections in this book, to continue carrying out the task that I was given by the Master—a task that now has for me the aura of an ancient prophecy—to "develop a grace."

I feel that the Lord is asking me to share again the *Letters of Tribulation*, to share them with all those who—in the midst of the confusion that the father of lies can sow in his persecutions—have decided to fight the good fight, free of the victimhood to which we are tempted to surrender and which, as we know, can hide in one's heart the inclination for revenge that does nothing but feed the evil it pretends to eliminate.

Faced with any temptation to confusion and defeatism, it is good for us to return, to feel the paternal spirit of those who preceded us and that animates these *Letters*. They teach us to choose consolation in moments of greatest desolation.

I recommend reading them and praying with them. These *Letters* are—and have been for many people at particular moments of life—a true source of gentleness, courage, and luminous hope.

8 November 2018

Francisco

Introduction

On Christmas day of 1987, Fr. Jorge Mario Bergoglio signed a short preface to a collection of eight letters from two superiors general of the Society of Jesus.[1] Seven were written between 1758 and 1773 by Father General Lorenzo Ricci, and the final one was written in 1831 by Father General Jan Roothaan. These texts reveal much about a great tribulation: the suppression of the Society of Jesus. With the apostolic brief *Dominus ac Redemptor* (July 21, 1773), Pope Clement XIV, under political pressure from various nations, suppressed the order. Subsequently, in August 1814, in the chapel of the Congregation of Nobles in Rome, Pope Pius VII promulgated the bull *Sollicitudo omnium Ecclesiarum*, formally and fully reestablishing the Society of Jesus.

In 1986, then-Fr. Bergoglio—following a period as provincial and then as rector of the Collegio Massimo and parish priest of San Miguel—was transferred to Germany for a year of study. After returning to Buenos Aires, he continued his studies and taught pastoral theology. Meanwhile, the Society of Jesus prepared for the Sixty-sixth Congregation of Procura-

---

1. *Las cartas de la tribulación* (Buenos Aires: Diego de Torres, 1988).

tors, which was held from September 27 to October 5, 1987. It was during this assembly that the Argentine province elected Bergoglio "procurator," a position that involved traveling to Rome with the tasks of reporting on the state of the province, discussing the conditions of the Society with other procurators elected by the various provinces, and voting on the possibility of holding a general congregation of the order.

It was in this context that Bergoglio decided to meditate on and republish the letters of Fathers Ricci and Roothaan, because, in his opinion, they were relevant and applicable to current issues facing the Society. To accompany their publication, he wrote a preface of just over three thousand words (half of which were comprised of a footnote) and signed it three months later.

Before the book was published, he discussed his preface with Fr. Miguel Ángel Fiorito, his spiritual father and a teacher and guide for a generation of Jesuits.[2] We make this preface available here again as the first article in this volume. It has long been unavailable and was published for the first time in Italian by *La Civiltà Cattolica*.[3] We also present the letters of the general superiors to which Bergoglio's text refers.

Since their publication in 1987, Francis has from time to time referred to these letters and to his own introductory reflection. For example, without his having made explicit reference to them, they clearly constituted the backbone of his important homily at the 2014 celebration of Vespers in the

---

2. José Luis Narvaja, "Miguel Ángel Fiorito and Popular Religiosity in the Context of Jorge Mario Bergoglio's Formation," *La Civiltà Cattolica* (July 2018). Available at https://www.laciviltacattolica.it/articolo/miguel-angel-fiorito/.

3. Jorge Mario Bergoglio, "The Doctrine of Tribulation," *La Civiltà Cattolica*, English ed. (May 2018).

INTRODUCTION

Church of the Gesù, on the occasion of the two-hundredth anniversary of the reestablishment of the Society of Jesus.

The most recent occasion of his having made reference to the letters was in a private conversation he had with Jesuits during his pastoral visit to Peru in 2018.[4] On this occasion, Francis called the letters of Fathers Ricci and Roothaan "a marvel of criteria of discernment, criteria of action to not allow ourselves to be dragged down by institutional desolation."

He made explicit reference to the letters again when he spoke to priests, consecrated men and women, and seminarians in Santiago de Chile on January 16, 2018. On that occasion, citing his own 1987 preface from the original publication of the letters, he encouraged his hearers to find the path to follow "when the tempest of persecutions, tribulations, doubts, and so forth, arises from cultural and historical events," and the temptation is to "keep dwelling on our own discouragement."[5]

Francis clearly wanted to offer a word to the church of Chile during a time of loss and a "whirlwind of conflicts." Again referring to these letters, he spoke about Peter. With the question "Do you love me?" Jesus wants to free Peter from "being upset by opposition and criticism. He wants to free him from being downcast and, above all, negative. With

---

4. Pope Francis, "Where Have Our People Been Creative? Conversations with Jesuits in Chile and Peru," *La Civiltà Cattolica* (February 2018). Available at https://www.laciviltacattolica.com/people-creative-conversations-jesuits-chile-peru/.

5. Pope Francis, Meeting with Priests, Consecrated Men and Women, and Seminarians, Santiago Cathedral (January 16, 2018). Available at http://www.vatican.va/content/francesco/en/speeches/2018/january/documents/papa-francesco_20180116_cile-santiago-religiosi.html.

his question, Jesus asks Peter to listen to his heart and learn how to *discern*." In short, "Jesus wants to save Peter from turning into someone who is a truthful destroyer or a charitable liar or a confused paralytic."[6] Jesus persists until Peter gives him a realistic answer: "Lord, you know everything; you know that I love you" (John 21:17). Thus Jesus confirms Peter in his mission. And, in this way, he definitively makes him his apostle.

These letters and the reflections that accompany them are important for understanding how Bergoglio himself feels he must act as the successor of Peter, that is, as Francis.

These are words that he speaks to the Church today, repeating them first of all to himself. And above all they are words that the pontiff considers essential today if the Church is to be able to face times of desolation, disturbance, and specious and anti-evangelical controversies.

What is the context of the new "letters of tribulation" offered in the second part of this book? After his trip to Chile and Peru (January 15–22, 2018), and rejecting the logic of "scapegoat," Francis took upon himself the responsibility and the "shame" of the scandal of the abuse of minors committed by clergy in Chile and the management of accusations of abuse. In this spirit, the pope returned to Rome and established a "Special Mission," led by Msgr. Charles J. Scicluna, to listen directly to the testimonies of victims and to collect documentation.

Following the visit to Chile and Special Mission's report, Pope Francis, in a letter dated April 8, 2018, summoned all the Chilean bishops to Rome to, in his words, "discuss the conclu-

---

6. Ibid.

sions of the aforementioned visit and my own conclusions."[7] It was precisely the publication of those letters thirty-one years previously that generated this new "letter of tribulation."

At the beginning of the meeting, which took place from May 15 to 17, 2018, the pope gave the bishops a new ten-page letter, which was not originally intended for publication but was made public by the Chilean television station TV 13. We offer here an English translation of that letter.

At the end of the meeting, Francis gave the bishops a brief public message and also entrusted to them a letter to "To the Pilgrim People of God in Chile," presented here in an English translation.

The second half of this book concludes with the pope's August 20, 2018, "Letter to the People of God," released after the publication of the grand jury report on pedophilia cases in the dioceses of Pennsylvania in the United States.

Letters of Tribulation represents an epistolary volume shaped over time in the context of difficult situations. It reveals a great deal about Francis and his way of dealing with times of desolation.

Francis's texts are accompanied here by helpful comments from two Jesuits: Fr. Diego Fares, of *La Civiltà Cattolica*, who has known the pontiff for a long time and who has accompanied him in times of desolation; and Fr. James Harney, of the University of Oxford, who wrote an insightful reflection regarding the "Letter to the People of God" on abuse.

In order to draw attention to the significance in the present moment of the texts he first ordered published in 1987,

---

7. Pope Francis, "Letter to the Bishops of Chile" following the report of Archbishop Charles J. Scicluna (April 8, 2018).

INTRODUCTION

Pope Francis agreed to compose a new preface for this book. "I feel that the Lord asks me to share again the *Letters of Tribulation*," he writes. He says the letters of the superiors general represent an important treatise on discernment in times of confusion and anguish, and that they express "the paternal spirit of those who preceded us and that animated [them]," inviting us to choose consolation.

They are thus interlinked in unity with the five letters written by Francis on tribulation in our own day.

The initial idea for this collection—a republication of the original 1987 booklet—occurred to me during the flight back from the pope's trip to Chile and Peru. It was later bolstered in light of the new "letters of tribulation" that the Pontiff wrote to the bishops of Chile and to the people of God. It took further shape in dialogue with Fr. Diego Fares, who prepared his commentary and, on November 8, 2018, finally received from Francis himself approval for publication as well as the preface in which he offers these texts—not only for our reading, but above all for our prayer.

Fr. Antonio Spadaro, SJ
Director, *La Civiltà Cattolica*

I

THE TRIBULATIONS OF YESTERDAY

The Doctrine of Tribulation

Jorge Mario Bergoglio, SJ

The texts that follow were written by two fathers general of the Society of Jesus: Fr. Lorenzo Ricci (elected general in 1758) and Fr. Jan Roothaan (elected in 1829). Both of them led the Society in difficult times of persecution. During the generalate of Fr. Ricci the suppression of the Society by Pope Clement XIV occurred.

For a long time the Bourbon courts were "demanding" that such a measure be taken. Pope Clement XIII [with the 1765 bull *Apostolicum Pascendi* – Ed.] confirmed the Institute founded by Saint Ignatius, but nevertheless the bashing of the Order by the Bourbon courts did not stop until the publication [by Clement XIV – Ed.] of the brief *Dominus ac Redemptor* in 1773 when the Society of Jesus was suppressed.[1]

---

1. There are various historical interpretations of the conduct of Pope Clement XIV. The point of view of each one of them is always based on some objective reality. I do not think that it is always right to absolutize a truth, transforming it into the only interpretative key. A good summary of this theme is found in G. Martina, *La Iglesia de Lutero a nuestros días,* 4 vols. (Madrid: Cristiandad, 1974, 2: 271–87). It also provides an abundant bibliography. The judgment that Ludwig Pastor makes regarding Clement XIV in his *History of the Popes* (Vol. 37) is extremely harsh. For example: "Clement XIV's weakness of character is the key to understanding his tactic of

Fr. Roothaan also experienced difficult times marked by liberalism and the entire current of the Enlightenment that gave rise to "modernity." In both cases, in that of Fr. Ricci and that of Fr. Roothaan, the Society was attacked mainly for its devotion to the Apostolic See: it was an indirect attack on the Church. Nevertheless, deficiencies were not lacking within the ranks of the Jesuits themselves.

It is not a matter here of going into more details about the history. What has been said is enough to frame this period of

---

conceding in everything possible to the demands of the Bourbon courts and by this means to restore peace..." (p. 90). "The most fatal quality of the new pope: weakness and timidity which were equaled by his deceit and mental slowness" (p. 82). "Pope Clement lacks courage and firmness; he is incredibly slow in resolving issues. He captivates people with pretty words and promises; he deceives and fascinates people. Initially he promises heaven and earth; later he raises difficulties and postpones the solution, in the Roman fashion, emerging triumphant in the end. In this way everyone gets caught in his net. He puts up a good appearance to avoid arriving at a decision in answer to the concerns of ambassadors; he dismisses them with nice words and cheerful hopes, which then are never realized. Whoever seeks to gain some favor had better try to do so at the first audience. Moreover, a perceptive ambassador can discover his underlying insincerity because he is so given to talk" (pp. 82–83). These are judgments that Pastor makes based on documents of the period, and while his opinion of Pope Ganganelli ends up being negative, his opinion of Ganganelli's secretary, Friar Bontempi, also a Conventual Franciscan, is much more negative. Pastor "charges" Bontempi with being practically the main person responsible for Ganganelli's errors. According to Pastor, Bontempi attempted to commit an act of simony by soliciting payment in return for the suppression of the Society. Bontempi succeeded in getting Clement XIV to name him a cardinal *in pectore*, but he failed to get his nomination made public when the pope was on his deathbed. Pastor presents Bontempi as an ambitious type without scruples who moves backstage behind the drapes and tries to be on "good relations with everyone" and thus prepares for his future.

the two fathers general. What is important is to realize that in both cases the Society of Jesus *experienced tribulation*, and the letters that follow are *the doctrine regarding tribulation* that both superiors recall for their members. They constitute a treatise about tribulation and how to endure it.

In times of disturbance, times in which the commotion of persecution, tribulations, doubts, and so forth arises as a result of cultural and historic events, it is not easy to discover the right road to follow. There are various temptations proper to such times: to argue over ideas, to not give to the matter the importance it should be given, to concentrate too much on the persecutors, to keep going over the desolation in one's mind, and the like.

In the following letters we see how both fathers general deal with such temptations, propose to the Jesuits a *doctrine* that forges them in their own spirituality,[2] and

---

2. Fr. Joseph de Guibert, SJ, in *The Jesuits: Their Spiritual Doctrine and Practice,* ed. George E. Ganns, SJ (Chicago: Institute of Jesuit Sources, 1964) states: "In accord with this (he refers to Decree 11 of the 19th General Congregation which elected Fr. Ricci as General of the Order) a series of poignant letters is found addressed by the new General to his religious men as the number of difficult situations piles up and dangers increase. On December 8, 1759, the day following Pombal's decrees destroying the Portuguese Provinces, he invites prayer for the immediate coming of the *spiritum bonum*, the true supernatural spirit of vocation, perfect docility to divine grace. Again on November 30, 1761, at the very moment when the storm reaches France, he asks that all one's trust be placed in God, that the trials be taken advantage of for the purification of souls, and that it be remembered that these trials bring us nearer to God and also serve for the greater glory of God. On November 13, 1763, he insists on the necessity of making prayer more effective through holiness of life, recommending above all humility, the spirit of poverty and the perfect obedience requested by St. Ignatius. On June 17, 1769, after the expulsion of the Spanish Jesuits, there is a new call

strengthen their belonging to the entire body of the Society. This belonging comes first and ought to prevail over all other memberships (in all kinds of institutions internal or external to the Society). This sense of belonging ought to characterize

---

to prayer and to zeal to purify oneself of minor defects. Finally, on February 22, 1773, six months before the signing of the brief *Dominus ac Redemptor,* in the face of a total lack of human assistance, Fr. Ricci wants to see the effect of God's mercy which invites those afflicted with trials to trust only in Him; he also exhorts the men to prayer, but only to ask for the preservation of a Society faithful to the spirit of its calling: 'If, God forbid, it should lose that spirit, its suppression would be of no importance, since it would have made itself useless for the purpose for which it was founded.' He finishes with a warm exhortation to maintain in their fullness the spirit of charity, of union, of obedience, of patience, and of evangelical simplicity. Such are the words with which Divine Providence wanted to close the spiritual history of the Society at that moment of supreme testing, of total sacrifice which would be demanded of it. Cordaro, and others after him, have criticized in Ricci an excessive passivity in the face of the attacks of which his Order was the object, a lack of energy and ability to take advantage of all the means at his disposal to frustrate the attacks. This is not the place to discuss whether such a criticism is well founded; but what are certainly preferable are invitations to hear repeated calls for supernatural fidelity, to holiness of life, and to the special grace of God in prayer as things that are essential at those final hours of the Order on the eve of death, rather than holding on to human abilities, legitimate, but without a doubt completely useless" (pp. 318–19). "There is hardly any need to recall the protest that Fr. Ricci near death took pains to read at the moment he received viaticum in the prison of *Castel Sant'Angelo* on November 19, 1775: at the moment of appearing before the tribunal of infallible truth, it was his duty to protest that the destroyed Society had given no reason for its suppression. He declared and gave witness to this with the certainty which a well-informed superior can morally possess regarding the state of his Order, as well as to not having himself given any motive whatsoever, no matter how small, for his imprisonment" (ibid., note 71).

any other commitment which, because of it, is transformed in "mission."[3]

Behind the cultural and sociopolitical stances of that epoch there is an underlying *ideology*: the Enlightenment, liberalism, absolutism, regalism, and so on. Nevertheless, what captures one's attention is how both fathers general—in their letters—do not attempt to "argue" with ideologies. They know full well that in such stances there are errors, lies, ignorance... Nevertheless, they leave those things aside and—in addressing the body of the Society—they center their reflection on *the confusion* that such ideas (and their cultural and political consequences) produce in the heart of Jesuits. It would appear that they feared the problem might not be properly approached. It is true that there was a struggle of ideas, but they preferred to go rather to life, to the situation that such ideas provoked.

Ideas are discussed; situations are discerned. These letters are meant to provide elements of discernment to Jesuits experiencing tribulation. Hence, in their arguments the superiors general prefer to mention confusion rather than error, ignorance, or lies. Confusion finds a place in the heart: it is the coming and going of diverse spirits. Truth or falsehood in the abstract is not the object of discernment. Confusion, however, is. Rather than argue about ideas, these letters *recall the doctrine*, and by means of it, lead the Jesuits *to take charge of their own vocation*.

Given the seriousness of those times and the ambiguity of specific situations, the Jesuit *ought to discern*, ought to pull himself together in terms of who he is as a member of the Society. He is not allowed to opt for any solutions that would

---

3. The 32nd General Congregation of the Society of Jesus, Decree 4, No. 66.

simply deny contrary and real polarities. He should seek to find *God's will* instead of an outcome that would leave him tranquil. The sign of his having discerned well would be found in peace (a gift of God), and not in the apparent tranquility of human equilibrium or of opting for an either/or.

Put in concrete terms, it is not of God to defend truth at the price of charity, nor charity at the price of truth, nor equilibrium at the price of both of them. In order to avoid becoming a truthful destroyer or a charitable liar or a confused paralytic, one needs to discern. It is the job of the superior to help in discernment. This is the deepest meaning of the letters that follow: an effort on the part of the head of the Society to help the body assume an attitude of discernment. This paternal attitude rescues the body from spiritual helplessness and rootlessness.

Finally, one more point about method. Recourse to the fundamental truths that give meaning to our membership or belonging appears to be the only way to properly approach discernment. Saint Ignatius recalls this whenever faced with a choice: "The focus of our intention ought to be simple, looking only at that for which [we are] created."[4] Moreover, it should not surprise us that in these letters the fathers general refer to the sins of Jesuits themselves, sins which, in a merely discursive but not discerning approach, would seem to have nothing to do with the external situation of confusion provoked by the persecutions.

What then happens is not a matter of chance. There is here a dialectic proper to the situational context of discernment—a dialectic that involves seeking interiorly within oneself a state of being similar to the external state. In

---

4. Cf. *Spiritual Exercises*, 169.

this case, seeing oneself solely as persecuted could engender the bad spirit of "feeling like a victim," like an object of injustice, for example. Outside, because of persecution, there is confusion... In considering his own sins the Jesuit asks for "shame and confusion for himself."[5] This is not the same thing, but it seems so; and in this way he is better disposed to do discernment.

Thus, with the letters that follow, we place in the hands of our readers this jewel of our spirituality.[6]

December 25, 1987

---

5. Ibid., 48.

6. *Epistolae Praepositorum Generalium ad Patres et Fratres Societatis Jesu,* Vol. 4, Rollarii, Iulii De Meester, 1909, 257–346. The letters that follow were translated from the original Latin by Fr. Ernesto Dann Obregón, SJ. (Ed. – In this volume the translation relies on both the Spanish and Italian editions.)

LETTERS OF THE SUPERIORS GENERAL
   OF THE SOCIETY OF JESUS
   TO THE FATHERS AND BROTHERS
   OF THE SOCIETY

LORENZO RICCI, SJ,
AND JAN ROOTHAAN, SJ

✝ LETTER OF M.R.P. [VERY REV. FATHER] LORENZO RICCI
TO THE FATHERS AND BROTHERS OF THE SOCIETY
September 26, 1758

*We must persevere in prayer
for the misfortunes that oppress and threaten the Society*

1. Even if, after praying to God very intensely, many misfortunes still oppress us and many still threaten us, we must not doubt God's mercy; indeed, we must in truth ascribe the situation to divine mercy, "for the Lord disciplines those whom he loves, and chastises every child whom he accepts" (Heb 12:6). God looks for and requests two things from us. The first is that we move toward virtue and love of religious perfection. He asks us for a more ardent devotion to him, thanks to which we take delight in being with him, and he also asks that we dedicate to prayer and holy meditation not only the time prescribed by our rule but also that which stems from our occupations and enables us to commit ourselves to increasing his glory in the tasks we undertake. He asks for a more ardent charity toward our neighbor, which leads us to wish no evil on anyone, to have no desire to blame or accuse anyone; indeed, it impels us to commit ourselves to be good to everyone, in every possible way. He calls for a greater commitment to developing those virtues that have to do with ourselves: mortification, which frees us from being absorbed in seeking our own comfort; humility, which engenders in us a modest opinion of ourselves and enables us to speak of ourselves modestly; poverty, which contents itself with what is necessary and rejects what is superfluous; prompt obedience, which makes no excuses. Having learned from letters that have come from various regions

of the fruits produced for many of us by our misfortunes, I say with the psalmist, "your rod and your staff—they comfort me" (Ps 23:4); our tribulations have filled me with joy, and I think nothing better could happen to us. May heaven grant that all of us obtain this same fruit and that each of us may say: "It is good for me that I was humbled, so that I might learn your statutes" (Ps 119:71).

2. But the merciful God has something else in mind too when he afflicts us, as those who know the ways of the Lord understand well. Certainly he is pleased with our prayers, our humility, the trust with which we take refuge in his heart; but he fears that if we are freed too quickly from our misfortunes, we will turn away from his presence. Therefore, my dearest Fathers and Brothers, listen to the voice of God who admonishes us with love, and do not hesitate to resort constantly to prayer.

3. But in order that our prayer may have greater efficacy, I would like it to be offered to God through the one who is most pleasing to him among all creatures, the one who is most powerful in obtaining grace. I refer to Mary, dearest Fathers and Brothers, whom in union with the Church we call, with deep affection, our advocate, our hope, the consolation of the afflicted. And since the most blessed Virgin is solicitous toward all those who turn to her with faith and piety, we trust that she will be mindful of us and extend to our Society her help and her care. When our holy father Ignatius prostrated himself at the altar to renounce his profane weapons, she inspired in him the idea of establishing a new militia; she welcomed into her embrace the Society, which was born on the day of her Assumption, and she bestowed on his disciples countless benefits. Therefore let us turn to her upon whom are hung "a thousand shields" (Song 4:4), or remedies against dangers, as Saint

LETTER TO THE FATHERS AND BROTHERS (SEPTEMBER 26, 1758)

Thomas explains, with which she drives away all fear and misfortune. Certainly the most holy Mother will not despise our prayers, but will turn her merciful eyes toward us.

4. I desire and I ask—and I do not doubt that each of you will respond willingly—that you commit yourselves to celebrating the next feast of the Immaculate Conception of the Blessed Virgin with particular devotion and that you precede it with a preparatory novena rich in devotions, as is the custom of holy men, asking the most loving Mother to stand in defense of our Society. I do not propose particular exercises for those days, since I might prescribe for you less than you are ready to do. I leave it to the decision of superiors to prescribe in our houses particular prayers or other pious exercises. However, I do not leave to anyone's decision but instead strongly recommend to all—and wish I could recommend to each one personally—a renewed devotion to the Divine Mother if perhaps it has diminished. From her will come all that is good, for each one of us and for the entire Society.

5. Therefore, dearest Fathers and Brothers, pray intensely to the most loving Mother, that she will show her special support for the Society, pouring out in all of us the spirit of her Son, and above all in me, who am the most needy of all, that I do no damage in any way either to the Company, whose government has been entrusted to me, or to my own soul. Please remember me in your Masses and prayers.

In Rome, September 26, 1758

The servant in Christ of you all, dearest Fathers and Brothers,

Lorenzo Ricci

LETTER OF M.R.P. LORENZO RICCI
TO THE FATHERS AND BROTHERS OF THE SOCIETY
December 8, 1759

*Constancy in prayer is needed
for the tribulations of the Society*

1. Last year, as you know, we implored divine mercy, praying intensely together, and in our afflictions we awaited heavenly consolation with humble hearts. I have no doubt that the Father of mercy looked kindly from heaven upon our prayers and tears, brought to him with the help of the angels. I feel too that the whole heavenly court was pleased by the spirit of humility and compunction with which we prostrated ourselves before the throne of God's grace. Even if we have been granted less than we asked, certainly our souls have been blessed with rest and other spiritual advantages.

2. This year, however, I feel that you yourselves have admonished me that we should not put a time limit on divine mercy, nor specify the day of his compassion. Instead, we must redouble our efforts in prayer until in our tribulation help arrives. It seems to me that you are tacitly asking me to enjoin on the entire Order new expiatory rites to contain heaven's wrath. And there is nothing I could do more willingly and nothing that could inspire more reverence in me than the thought of the day and the hour in which the whole Society stands before God and raises to him the cry of the humble, which penetrates heaven and is always pleasing to God—

the offering of a contrite and humble heart, which he never despises.

3. And this is certainly so, dearest Fathers and Brothers. Divine benefits are bestowed in response to the perseverance of those prayers that are humble, fervent, and full of trust. Judith spoke a great truth: "Know that the Lord will answer your prayers if you persevere in fasting and praying before God" (Jdt 4:12 Vg). Be certain, then, that in the end you will obtain the mercy of the most loving Father, provided that you do not distance yourselves from his presence and that, overcome by boredom and fatigue, you do not grow slack in your pious duty of prayer. It is in fact the nature of him who is magnanimous to be touched by the cries of the unfortunate who implore his help. Divine mercy, in truth, by its nature, is inclined to ease the worries of mortals. And finally, he who can never fail in fidelity to his promises clearly urges us to be constant in asking, in requesting, in knocking, in order to obtain what we need: "Ask, and it will be given you; search, and you will find; knock, and the door will be opened for you" (Mt 7:7; cf. Jn 16:24).

4. Christ himself demonstrates the efficacy of persevering in prayer, and he demonstrates it in such a sweet way. Anyone who is dedicated to reading Saint Luke cannot fail to nurture in his soul a certain trust. We are told that men are won over by the nuisance of some friend who implores them, and that among you there is no kind-hearted father who is so harsh and cruel as not to be persuaded by the prayers of a child who begs and prays. If, therefore, the earnestness and perseverance of prayers are so effective in the context of men, who by nature are generally inclined to evil, how much

more effective will they be in relation to God, whose nature is goodness, whose generosity is not exhausted by gifts, for whom our supplications are not annoying but pleasing and a source of joy, and finally, than whom no friend is more sincere and no father more loving? "If you then, who are evil, know how to give good gifts to your children, how much more will the heavenly Father give the Holy Spirit to those who ask him" (Lk 11:13).

5. In short, I would like you to seek diligently, with your prayers, above all that *good spirit* of which he himself speaks: obviously the spirit of penance and compunction for recognized sins; the spirit of charity, zeal, and untiring commitment to the salvation of souls; the spirit of humility and mortification, of contempt for the world and for ourselves; the spirit of piety and devotion to God and of perfect submission to his will; the spirit of right obedience; but, above all, the "spirit of compassion and supplication," as the scripture says (Zech 12:10), in which alone is contained every excellent and perfect gift. In summary, I would like you to seek that spirit which God infused from the beginning into this Society of his, with which he has kept it ever since and has sustained it to this day.

6. Do not be surprised that I am so solicitous with regard to this particular spirit, as if we did not have to ask insistently for anything else. In fact, whether you look at its distinction or at the gifts that flow from it, it is such an excellent good that in its light all other goods are deminished. Moreover, the heavenly Father knows well the other needs that oppress us, and he himself promises to those who seek the kingdom of God above all that he will also give all other goods. Finally,

no one can doubt that God orders his decisions toward us especially for this purpose: to remove from us anything that leads us to exclude that spirit of which I spoke, and indeed, that that same spirit in us be awakened and become more vigorous. When that happens, we can certainly hope that in other things the divine goodness will be propitious toward us.

7. Therefore, for these reasons I refer you to the words of the Apostle: "Do not quench the Spirit" (1 Thes 5:19). God in his kindness will certainly grant you the light of the Spirit; and once it is lit, do not snuff it out, either through neglect in what concerns devotion, or through dealing lazily with your duties, or through immoderately desiring the comforts of worldly life, of fame, or of any other vain or perishable things. Everyone must open his heart docilely to the divine voice from which he will easily understand what God asks of him. Each one must fear putting some obstacle in the way of heavenly grace and causing, through his own faults, public calamities.

8. Most beloved ones, your prayers must also take into account the other needs of our Order, as Christ teaches us and as is the custom of the Church. But first we must recognize, with due humility, that our misfortunes are to be attributed to our faults. And let us accept these misfortunes humbly, as given by the divine hand, who chastens us paternally. With this attitude, which touches the very heart of God's mercy, raise your hands and your voices to heaven. The merciful Father will listen, as is his wont, to the requests of the downcast. And if these prayers have too little efficacy, ask in the name of the one who is our mediator with the Father and intercedes with his merits for us. Nothing is denied to those who ask in

his name. And since with Christ the prayers of the saints, and above all those of his most blessed Mother, have great value, call upon them to help, ask them to intercede for you. Pray to the Virgin Mary with the words of the Church, that she may show herself to be mother and that she may offer with her own hands your prayers to him who, having decided to be born for us, deigned to be born of her.

9. I therefore mandate that in the nine days that precede the Annunciation (if this letter has not been delivered to you in time, choose any feast day in honor of the Blessed Virgin) all shall prepare for such feast with special exercises of piety that shall be established by the individual superiors and in which, to the extent possible, everyone will take part together. This is to be in addition to personal prayers and voluntary mortifications that each one will undertake according to his decision, or rather, according to the ardor of his devotion, after having consulted his own spiritual director. Further, for the whole of the next year, 1760, all priests shall celebrate a Mass each week for our Society in addition to the usual one; and I truly wish this Mass be celebrated by all on the same day, which could be a Saturday. In addition, at all Masses there shall be added the collect "For the Congregation and Family." Finally, those who are not priests are to recite every week one rosary for the Society in addition to the rosary prescribed by the rule.

10. It only remains for me to pray and beseech all and every one, which I do from the depths of my soul, to ask God to give me that spirit that I ask him to give others; that I do not through my faults draw divine punishment on the Society, which does not deserve it. I also ask you to pray that God

LETTER TO THE FATHERS AND BROTHERS (DECEMBER 8, 1759)

may be my light, my strength, and my salvation and that he direct my steps before him: for this above all I entrust myself with all my strength to your holy Masses and your prayers.

In Rome, December 8, 1759

Lorenzo Ricci

LETTER OF M.R.P. LORENZO RICCI
TO THE FATHERS AND BROTHERS OF THE SOCIETY
November 30, 1761

The reasons for consolation and recourse to God

1. In the many and great misfortunes by which our Society is oppressed, according to the just and merciful will of God, my fear, dearest Fathers and Brothers, is not that you endure serious damage because of their strength and number, but that your spirit falter and turn away from endurance and trust in God. In thinking about that fear I suddenly remembered the psalm that says, "our destiny is in your hands" (Ps 31:15), that is, in the hands of the most loving Father. Nothing happens without his approval, and all things are ordered by him for our benefit and spiritual growth. Everything derives from his infinite love for us.

2. And from this single source flow innumerable reasons for consolation. As the prophet says, "Many are the afflictions of the righteous" (Ps 34:19). This being the case, we should rejoice because the divine kindness calls us, though unworthy and sinners, to the fate of the just. And our consolation should not be any less at the thought that God has allowed [the tribulation] as not so much an exercise for virtue as a punishment for our sins. This, in fact, is proper to divine mercy. He, *who in the time of tribulation forgives the sins of those who call upon him* (Tb 3:13 Vg), prescribes punishments in this life, in which we serve much lighter penalties for our sins. Our endurance of

the pain of this bears the fruit of a great merit, and does not preserve punishement for the other life in which, although sins are repented with the pain of far worse penalties, yet endurance of that pain is devoid of any usefulness of merit. Therefore if our life, as it is written in the third chapter of Tobit, "be on trial, it will be crowned; and if it is under correction, it will be allowed to reach the mercy of God" (Tb 3:21 Vg).

3. God's purpose is not simply to substitute lighter and more helpful sufferings for very hard and less useful sufferings; it is also to prepare us to obtain very great rewards in heaven, but on condition of bearing the tribulations, given by himself, with patience and humbly, in a word, in imitation of Christ the Lord and of the Saints. This, in fact, is the narrow and hard road that leads to life (cf. Mt 7:14), and the narrower the path we follow, the more joyful that life will be. The tribulations have a price, with which, so to speak, we acquire immense glory, and the more lavishly we pay the price, the greater the glory we will gain.

4. To attain this end, then, no instrument is more suitable than tribulation. It is like fire, purifying our sentiments and purging them of every dishonor and every vice. In fact, if in the labors we undertook for the glory of God and the salvation of souls we were tacitly looking for some advantage or for human praise—something that can easily happen because of our fallen nature and the wiles of our common enemy—in tribulation we find that our expectations were not met, that we were denied the goods we sought, which were in any case vain. Then, driven by a holy desperation, we recall our soul from all earthly things and we learn to refer everything to God, whose fidelity we cannot doubt.

5. When our miserable life becomes boring to us, we raise our minds to a longing for our heavenly homeland. The blindness and the vanity of our nature are attracted more by the presence of a vain good than by the hope of a true future good. For this reason, when life has nothing of that vain good but instead is tormented by worries, fear, and sorrows, the experience teaches us that there is nothing left but to desire that blessed homeland in which, when we set foot, "God will wipe away every tear from [our] eyes" (Rev 7:17).

6. Further, tribulation is useful in that it makes us humble and cautious in acting and in speaking, and it ignites a love for prayer. Just as praise, applause, favor, and esteem arouse the pride inherent in the souls of men, so too contempt, offense, abandonment, and any wounding of our pride make us aware of our smallness and do not allow us to crave what we cannot have. When we realize that others are watching us closely, intent on reproaching us, criticizing us, eager to accuse us and strip us of everything that belongs to us, we start being careful with our words and actions so as not to provide opportunities for others to slander us. Finally, since we cannot escape our difficulties with human help, we raise our eyes to God. We invoke more often and with greater ardor the One who "does not delight in our being lost, but after a storm brings peace, and after tears and weeping pours out rejoicing" (Tb 3:22 Vg).

7. God certainly sees our tribulations from heaven. If we bear them in a manner befitting the servants of God, he rejoices in the triumph that is not so much ours as his, his victory in us through grace. With God the saints rejoice, and they await us as future companions in consolation, just as we are of one an-

other now in suffering. In fact, God makes use of tribulations —"the repeated blows of the salutary hammer," as the Church sings [in the hymn of the Divine Office for the Dedication of a Church]—to form in us the image and the likeness of his Son Jesus Christ, to be brought to completion in the glory of blessed eternity.

8. I add another consideration for your comfort, which is essential for those who love God. No one may doubt that our tribulations, whatever they may be, whatever their causes and whatever their outcome, will serve the glory of God. So there is no reason for these tribulations to make us us anxious, since we seek the greater glory of God in everything, according to the rule of our Society. For us it is enough that from our tribulations God be honored. It is good that in the midst of them we be tranquil, indeed— if we truly love God—that we even rejoice in them.

9. These are the consolations with which "the Father of mercies and the God of all consolation... consoles us in all our affliction" (2 Cor 1:3–4). As I meditate on these things, trusting that you, dearest Brothers, will obtain those most abundant fruits of which I have spoken, I feel that if I had the soul of the saints, with the Apostle I would say: "I am overjoyed in all our affliction" (2 Cor 7:4). And if ever it were pleasing to God to obtain from us the correction of our shortcomings in this way, to increase in us the fear of him, to promote the observance of the rule, the passion for prayer, humility, charity, mortification, contempt for the world, and zeal for souls, I would ask him not to remove the hand from the whip, and it would be for me a consolation that he not spare me from the pain, as long as these fruits of tribulation persist in our Society.

10. As for the rest, while I am distressed by this and by my weakness and overwhelmed by the sorrow of the present evils and by fear of future ones, most of all I fear that you will stop enduring and being confident. Certainly God does not allow our tribulations to be endless, since he is touched by compassion for our suffering, because "he knows how we were made" (Ps 103:14) and acts toward us like a father, one whose love immediately restrains the hand from punishing the son, so that he may "give glory to his own name" (Jdt 7:24 Vg) and act toward us "according to [his] abundant mercy" (Ps 51:1).

11. And in truth it is not difficult to implore divine mercy. As long as you hope for it in a way worthy of the divine goodness and power, as far as is possible, we are safe. Who of you, in fact, does not know that, as the scriptures explain, the reason the afflicted are delivered from evil is that they have hoped in God? "He will...save them because they hoped in him," says the prophet (Ps 36:40 Vg), and again: "Because I hoped in you, Lord, you answered me" (Ps 37:16 Vg), and elsewhere: "Because he hoped in me I will deliver him" (Ps 90:14 Vg). Who has not heard those words: God "is the shield of all that hope in him" (2 Sam 22:31 Vg; cf. Ps 17:31 Vg); "He does not knock down those who trust, but raises up those who hope in the Lord, surrounding them with mercy" (Sir 32:28; cf. Pr 29:25; Ps 31:10 Vg). But who would fear the evils that besiege us if with his faith he knew that divine mercy surrounds us? Finally, it is not possible to read without great emotion those words of the second chapter of Ecclesiasticus and the second chapter of the first book of the Maccabees, where we are called to look at all the nations and peoples and to understand that "no one has hoped in the Lord and been confounded" (Sir 2:11 Vg) and to see that

"none of those who put their trust in him will lack strength" (1 Mc 2:61). What we see in every nation and generation, our experience also teaches us. Think back on all the times that God freed from evil our predecessors, who had been oppressed by calamities, because they hoped in him. If we are not enduring anything similar or worse, it follows that our hope must be stronger than that of our predecessors, since "in the sight of heaven there is no difference between saving by many or by few" (1 Mc 3:18). Therefore let us "approach the throne of grace with boldness" (Heb 4:16). Let us call upon God "out of [our] distress" (Ps 118:5) and he will hear us. He will save us "out of mighty waters" (2 Sam 22:17), for God "can save from every danger" (Wis 14:4; cf. Jb 36:15) and he "is rich in mercy" (Eph 2:4).

12. While in past years I have asked you to pray, this year I do so even more insistently because of the greater the misfortunes that oppress us and assail us. I would willingly endure all the years of my tenure being years of tribulation as long as these same years are years of supplication and prayer. I am sure that God will never deprive us of his mercy, as long as he does not deprive us the of spirit of prayer, as the Psalm says: "Blessed be God, because he has not rejected my prayer or withheld his steadfast love from me" (Ps 66:20).

13. For the next year, I have decided to suggest to you—indeed, to entrust you with—three exercises of piety. The first is that everyone, every day, approach the Most Blessed Sacrament and there, devoutly implore divine favor for our Society. Even in cases in which this cannot be done everywhere and by everyone together at a specific time, I would have to question the piety of individuals who fail to do it,

unless that failure is due to some just impediment. All should be aware that the misfortune we are dealing with concerns everyone. They should consider how much they are indebted to the Society, which nourishes them in virtue. They should make sure that for the sin of some the entire Society does not continue to suffer. The second exercise is that the litany of the blessed Virgin be recited before that of the saints, which is normally recited every day. The third is that for three days before each of the five solemn feasts of the blessed Virgin, the observance of which are church precepts, in all our houses everyone should pray for at least half an hour before an image or a relic, either in the house chapel or privately in the church. Furthermore, those with greater piety who are not content with these simpler practices may add other prayers, personal sacrifices, and works of devotion. Before the Father and his Son Jesus Christ we must implore intercessors and advocates: first of all the most blessed Virgin, about whom it has never been felt that she abandoned anyone who sought her help; then also the holy guardian angels of our Society, Saint Joseph and Saint John Nepomucene,[1] whom we chose as our special patrons; and those who while alive enriched the Society with their virtues and who now protect it from heaven. When intercessors are multiplied, God gives us his favor in abundance.

14. Finally, I would diligently warn you that help in tribulation is promised not to the prayers and words of anyone, but to the just. In fact "The eyes of the Lord are on the righteous,

---

1. [Ed. note: St. John Nepomucene (d. 1393), confessor to the Queen of Bohemia, was drowned at the behest of King Wenceslaus of Bohemia when he refused to divulge secrets of the confessional.]

and his ears are open to their cry... When the righteous cry for help, the Lord hears, and rescues them from all their troubles... I sought the Lord, and he answered me, and delivered me from all my fears" (Ps 33:16, 18, 5). Remember that hope belongs to those who fear the Lord, as it is said: "You who fear the Lord, hope in him" (Sir 2:9 Vg). "Trust in the Lord, and do good" (Ps 37:3). Thus, so that your hope may be steadfast and your prayers may be effective, do good, pursue justice, seek and fear God with that filial fear that is horrified by slightest offense against the Father. Direct your steps according to the most holy laws of obedience. Make it your aim to achieve the goal that the most loving Father has proposed, so that through our tribulations we may grow in holiness and our love of virtue may increase.

15. I have written these lines to offer you some consolation, confident that nothing is more certain or more firm, and also to soothe my own sorrow, which is intensified by yours. I conclude with the words of the Apostle, which complete what I have said to you: I ask you to "serve the Lord. Rejoice in hope, be patient in suffering, persevere in prayer" (Rom 12:11–12). Finally, turning to heaven, I pray that "the God of hope fill you with all joy and peace" (Rom 15:13), and I beseech you to remember me in your prayers and at Mass.

In Rome, November 30, 1761

Your servant in Christ,

Lorenzo Ricci

LETTER OF M.R.P. LORENZO RICCI
TO THE FATHERS AND BROTHERS OF THE SOCIETY
November 13, 1763

*On ardent perseverance in prayer
during the misfortunes of the Society*

1. Although the ongoing harshness of our misfortunes alone is enough to exhort us to a fervent perseverance in prayer, nevertheless "I think it right, as long as I am in this body, to refresh your memory" (2 Pt 1:13). I do this both because divine providence orders us to be humble but diligent seekers and interpreters of his intentions, and because this public tribulation torments some perhaps less than it should, since their personal comfort is in only a minor or in no way disturbed. There are others who, concentrating only on visible misfortunes, fail to raise their eyes toward the invisible hand that allows these tribulations. Indeed, it also happens that, when the weight of the tribulation increases daily, the continuity of the evil can actually give rise to a certain numbness. This can happen because repetition does not move us, or because we become accustomed to the pain and lose all hope of finding a remedy for it.

2. Far from us, dearest Fathers and Brothers, be this dullness of heart! On the one hand, it would frustrate God's paternal plans, and on the other, it would deprive us of the reward for patience. It would impede us in our exercises of piety, exercises that, if used incessantly and faithfully, would ultimately be of

such great value in terms of divine mercy that they themselves would transform our sadness into joy. For this reason, we must never—to use the words of the Apostle—forget the consolation (cf. Heb 12:5 Vg) of the words with which God, reproaching us as beloved children, exhorts us to endure: "My child, do not despise the Lord's discipline or be weary of his reproof" (Prv 3:11). It is not good that the serenity of mind with which the tribulation must be borne be disturbed or diminished by the tribulation itself. In fact, "It is right to be subject to God; mortals should not think that they are equal to God" (2 Mc 9:12). The tribulation, as it comes from God, is therefore pleasing to him. This must be enough for us, so that not only may it be borne by each of us with tranquility and submission but also that it may please us, obviously putting our will in accord with the divine will. In fact, what can we will, wisely and usefully, if not what God himself wills? And what could please us, other than what pleases God?

3. But this consent of our will with the divine will does not put an end to our pain, a pain of which we are particularly aware in our spiritual life. And yet, what offering of gratitude could be made to God by one who, through the habit of suffering, has lost all sensation of pain? Even divine help does not extinguish the pain that is proper to suffering. This pain makes us strong and constant, alleviating our interior afflictions with an ineffable sweetness, so that before the riches of heavenly delights it makes these words of the Apostle spring forth in the holy soul: "I am filled with consolation; I am overjoyed in all our affliction" (2 Cor 7:4).

4. As for the rest, just as Christian conformity to the divine will does not detract from the bitter pain of suffering, so it

must not take anything away from the fervor of our prayer. Christ, who is our true teacher, after having uttered this humble prayer: "Let your will be done as in heaven, so on earth," immediately added: "Give us today our daily bread," so as to teach us that we must pray to the Father even for help of a temporal kind.

5. Therefore, dearest Fathers and Brothers, while we await "from the Lord, who made heaven and earth" (Ps 120:2) the help that we will never receive from anywhere else, let us again have recourse to him. The groans of our hearts rise to the throne of his grace; let us not tire of exclaiming: "Turn, O Lord! How long? Have compassion on your servants!" (Ps 90:13). We should not tire, I say again, praying with even greater fervor, that he may be indulgent, if not because of our merits then at least because of his benevolence; that by the constant prayers and sighs of his servants he may be moved to hear and answer. To this end I desire and mandate that we all commit ourselves again in the coming year to the same devotional exercises of the years past, reciting daily the litanies of the blessed Virgin Mary, observing a triduum of prayer before each of her feasts, and making daily visits to the Blessed Sacrament.

6. These exercises are truly simple, suitable for promoting personal piety, and also sweet. For who does not find it sweet to invoke Mary? For whom is the presence of Jesus Christ not most sweet? There is no reason for me to fear that any of you would neglect these practices. But it is good to remember that our prayers are all the more pleasing to God, all the more efficacious in moving him to mercy, if they are accompanied by our efforts to grow ever more holy in morals and perfect in virtue: "When the righteous cry for help," says the royal poet,

"the LORD hears, and rescues them from all their troubles" (Ps 34:17); and in Proverbs one reads, "The Lord... hears the prayer of the righteous" (Prv 15:29). What can we say, given the fact that we ourselves imitate or follow the example of the faithful when we seek the help of others in prayer: we turn with greater confidence to those who demonstrate greater holiness of life. Let us choose advocates for ourselves from among those whom we consider most pleasing to God, ignoring those who are only nominally members of the family of Christ and are not known for being particularly virtuous.

9 [sic]. Furthermore, I strongly desire that your prayers be adorned and equipped with this characteristic, namely, sanctity of behavior. Although it can be considered something external to prayer, yet prayer draws all its intrinsic strength from it. It is thus proper for one who is not lukewarm, not submissive, but pious and holy, to weave into his prayer humility, trust, and perseverance. If each and every single member of the Society were fervent in coming before God, if every one of us were to see himself as God's close friend, then, I ask you, could there be anything that would be too great to ask of God, that the prayers of the entire Society would not be able to obtain from his divine goodness? How fast our prayer would fly to the throne of God, how certain it would be to produce blessings if, at the time of daily adoration of the Most Blessed Sacrament or of the recitation of the litanies, all the members of our Order were to pray as one. And what if, at the same time, those who sincerely abhor what the world loves and embraces—pleasures, great fame, honors—and seek and desire what Christ has loved and embraced, that is, contempt, poverty, and pain; those whose greatest and most intense commitment is to seek greater abnegation in everything;

those who are moved by right intention not only with regard to their state of life but also with regard to all particular things; those who are ready to respond immediately to the slightest sign from the superior indicating where the greater glory of God is calling; finally, those who burn with that "fire" that Christ "came to bring... to the earth" (Lk 12:49); what if all these were to pour out their prayers? You yourselves decide: could it happen that God, who hears the prayers even of a single believer, would not hear the prayers of so many men devoutly making their plea to him?

10. When we pray, the characteristics mentioned above should be ours. They are the characteristics that flow from the principal foundations of our Society, to whose observance we must dedicate ourselves intensely. I know that the same perfection may not be demanded or expected of every individual in the Society; yet I also know that much can be asked of every individual according to the measure of grace he has received. Certainly everyone has been blessed abundantly with divine grace. Furthermore, everyone is under the same rule of life, so that all may aspire to the highest possible degree of perfection. But I am aware, with sorrow, that in a large family of religious, both because of circumstances and because of the weak nature of men, there will be some who are lukewarm and lax. I know that this is inevitable, for, as Christ declared, "occasions for stumbling are bound to come" (Mt 18:7). But to these lukewarm men, especially those who, as Jerome says, by their sin make what is inevitable in the world happen through them, to these I say, it is important that you call to mind these words of Christ himself and determine to seriously meditate on them: "Woe to the one by whom the stumbling block comes!" (Mt 18:7).

11. To be more precise: it is good to devote ourselves to three types of virtue, which I recommend above all others. This not because I propose to talk about them extensively, but because they offer practical help in obtaining the benefits that we seek. God wills that some cultivate these virtues more perfectly, ready to grant our prayers if they are cultivated with care, according to his will.

12. We begin then with humility. You well know, dearest Fathers and Brothers, that God calls us and has called us and destined us to procure and promote his glory through the work of his servant Ignatius. But if, putting the glory of God aside, our commitment sets as its sole purpose the individual glory of each one of us, who among us could so foolishly delude ourselves to hope that God will paternally watch over our Society or that the very founder of the Society, Ignatius, will solicitously beg the divine majesty to preserve his work? Then surely our Society would become that "salt" that "has lost its taste," which "is no longer good for anything, but is thrown out and trampled under foot" (Mt 5:13).

13. And let us not deceive ourselves about the good repute of the Society. It is obvious that it must be defended and actively promoted, but only for the greater good of the neighbor and that it may give greater glory to God. We must foster the good reputation of the Society with purity of behavior, holiness of words, tireless passion for the salvation of souls—certainly not with ostentatious praise of its merits, or with backbiting, or with contempt for others. Furthermore, it is to be feared that under a commendable, thin mantle of care for the Society's reputation there may lurk a hidden and perverse desire for one's personal interest. For

example, we might take pleasure in the Society's prestige if, as often happens, it is the result of some action we have taken and, conversely, we may dismiss the prestige resulting from the actions of others, a prestige that has no personal advantage for us.

14. It is easy to say, "For the Greater Glory of God." If only it were as easy to act for the glory of God with no whiff of vainglory! Whoever wants to act purely for the glory of God must despise his own advantage. He must put aside any concern for personal honor to the point of forgetting himself, intent only on God. Finally, we will never pray to God with a sincere heart or glorify his holy name if we do not pray together with David that glory not be ours: "Not to us, O Lord, not to us, but to your name give glory" (Ps 115:1).

15. The second virtue that can lead us to achieve the goal of our prayers is poverty. It is proper to Christ, who "though he was rich, yet for your sakes he became poor" (2 Cor 8:9), so much so that he gave life to the religious institutions inspired by the evangelical precepts of voluntary poverty: "Blessed are the poor in spirit" (Mt 5:3)! It thus follows that the disciples of Christ must be recognized by their poverty as if it were of their essence; even the apostles described their vocation as his followers and companions with the words: "Look, we have left everything and followed you" (Mt 19:27). It is right and good that our prayers arrive in heaven in the same spirit, that Saint Ignatius may acknowledge them as those of his children and not of strangers and offer them to the Holy Spirit to obtain a good outcome, so that Christ in the end may assume guardianship of his Society, adorned and pleasing to him because of its genuine spirit of poverty.

16. Although we have committed ourselves to the imitation of Christ with poverty of spirit, that commitment could be restricted to narrower boundaries. If our poverty does not go beyond privations in owning things and submission to superiors with regard to the use of things, then we will not fully experience what poverty really means. In fact, if, after having kissed the wounds of the crucified Christ, after having wept tears of commiseration for the suffering Christ, we turn again to him and compare our poverty to his, then we must lower our faces in shame. This has been the experience of many holy souls who have been closer than we are to the crucified Christ.

17. But our poverty should at least reach the point of enduring without complaint if we are deprived of something. Be content with the usual standard of life in the Society and with the goods that, as the rule prescribes, image the goods of the poor. Maintain in all things a religious simplicity; reject always whatever is a source of secular luxury and worldly pleasure; refrain from every excess; desire nothing beyond what is necessary; distance yourself from and consider superfluous all that is outside of our habits of life. Arriving at this level of perfection—which all ought to achieve, since it is an undertaking that is neither too high nor too difficult—will be easy if, by carefully mediating on that poverty which Christ did not consider a disgrace to embrace, we arouse in our own hearts a love for it.

18. The third virtue is perfect obedience. Saint Ignatius wanted this to be the distinctive sign of the Society that would distinguish it from other religious families. Of this virtue I would not presume to speak, since the founder of the Society

himself in a marvelous letter has so clearly described its nature, distinguished its degrees, taught ways of practicing it, demonstrated how to obtain it, and provided strong and sure exhortations inviting us to exercise it perfectly. Therefore, I consider it sufficient for me to caution you, in passing, not to incur any fault in something so assuredly critical.

19. The blessed father points out that it is in no way prohibited to confer with one's superior in case there are differences of opinion; and the Constitutions clearly state that all are permitted to notify the superior if they feel that something is detrimental to them or if they have some special need with regard to food, clothing, work, or housing. Dearest Fathers and Brothers, you have every right to enjoy this legitimate, paternal, and prudent indulgence. I beg you, however, never to ignore the precautions that limit its use. In fact you know, as Ignatius himself teaches, that there is a great danger of selfishness in every manifestation of one's personal judgment that differs from a superior's orders. Therefore we need to ask the Father who gives us light whether it is useful to address the superior on a particular matter. Our prayer should be neither superficial nor anxious, but meek and open to listening to and accepting the voice of God, taking care not to confuse our own desires with the will of God. Before and after presenting one's own opinion, it is necessary to have that serenity of mind spoken of by the holy founder, not only with regard to the execution and the will, but also with regard to the judgment itself. This indifference will not seem difficult to those who see the will of God in the orders of the superior.

20. As to those of you who may be contemplating making some complaint against the rule of obedience, other texts of

Saint Ignatius come to mind. Be aware that it is clearly taught by him that we must not oppose, or contradict, or even give the slightest hint of disagreement between us and the superior; we must not wait for the superior's order to be spoken, but rather we must quickly obey the slightest indication of his will; we must not struggle to bend his will to ours, but rather we must allow him free disposition of us and our goods; we must conform our will to what he wants and thinks in all things—as long as sin is not involved, which is always to be understood. And when it happens that he gives us orders that are difficult and repugnant to our sensibility, even then we must obey readily, forcefully, with due humility, without excuses or murmurs.

21. This brings to mind Ignatius's use of the images of an old man's staff and a corpse,[1] with the latter illustrating the docility of the truly obedient religious. Also brought to mind as inspiring and admirable examples are those ancient monks whose will and efforts were engaged in undertaking, by order of the superior, tasks that were not only useless but even impossible.

22. Finally, when it comes to opposing the thought of the superior, recall those wise and gentle reasons Saint Ignatius offers in urging us to perfect obedience. He says that religious should be ashamed to obey for some human purpose. God keep you from such a futile and vile reason to act; the only

---

1. [In his *Constitutions*, St. Ignatius illustrated authentic obedience by offering the images of a corpse, which can be moved around without offering the least resistance, and an old man's staff, which serves whatever purpose is wished by the one who holds it. See *Constitutions*, n. 547. – Trans.]

reason for obedience is the love of God. Return to him, through full obedience, the freedom he has given to you. What is given by God does not die, but becomes perfect. In truth, we profess and pronounce our obedience more to God than to man, since man is nothing but the minister of God, a living instrument through which the divine will is expressed to us. The Holy Spirit clearly preaches obedience in the sacred scriptures; God himself approved of it at times with miracles; all the saints have exercised it; even our Lord Jesus Christ himself embraced it and left us admirable examples of it. Perfect obedience will sow in your mind all the other virtues. It will bind you all with the sweet and mutual bond of charity. It will produce that quiet and exultation of soul that those who are not docile do not know and will never know. It will smooth the way to progress in virtue in the service of God; it will bring you to the true knowledge of God, to the true love that will govern you and lead you on this pilgrimage of life and bring you to a most blessed end, to eternal beatitude.

23. Without any doubt, dearest Fathers and Brothers, you know not only the thoughts but also the very words of your most loving father, I mean Ignatius, whose only passion while he was alive was to lead each of you to a high degree of glory in heaven. From the throne of heavenly splendor that he occupies he prays for you and intercedes for you, as he did when in this world, that you may with all your strength commit yourselves in obedience and that you may excel in this virtue. Never lose sight of his sweet exhortation and his memory. Rather, keep them before your eyes—especially when you feel antipathy toward the orders of your superior—and they will certainly keep you safe from every mistake and deception in your thinking.

24. Accompany your prayers not only with these virtues but also with other virtues that can serve as intermediaries, so to speak, before the throne of God. If we do not unite these virtues with our prayers, we will, like Jeremiah, be setting up between us and God a very dense cloud, because of which our own prayers will be intercepted and rejected: "You have wrapped yourself with a cloud so that no prayer can pass through" (Lam 3:44). Our prayer, on the contrary, is filled with all these virtues, and so will be a prayer that, as James the apostle says, "is powerful and effective" (Jam 5:16). In fact it will be the prayer of those "righteous" ones whose "salvation," as the Holy Spirit says, "is from the Lord," for whom God is a refuge "in the time of trouble" (Ps 37:39), from whom he does not avert his eyes, whose paths he preserves (cf. Prv 2:20), whose home he blesses (cf. Prv 3:33), whose steps he directs, and whose weakness he strengthens. Dearest Fathers and Brothers, let us prepare to pray, and pray even more, to obtain these virtues for me and for all the companions, the better to ward off tribulation. We will always be happy with our fate if with the Apostle we can bear this witness: "Whether we live or whether we die, we are the Lord's" (Rom 14:8). I entrust myself particularly to your prayers and to your remembrance at Mass.

Rome, November 13, 1763

Dearest Reverend Fathers and Dear Brothers, I am,
Yours in Christ,

Lorenzo Ricci

LETTER OF M.R.P. LORENZO RICCI
TO THE FATHERS AND BROTHERS OF THE SOCIETY
January 16, 1765

*Confirmation of our Institute
by His Holiness Clement XIII*

1. I send you a copy of the most recent Apostolic Constitution [*Apostolicum pascendi*, issued January 12, 1765] with which the Most Holy Father, Pope Clement XIII, affirming the divine right of the Holy Roman See and having had mercy on our misfortunes by virtue of his extraordinary kindness toward the afflicted, renews the approval and confirmation of our Society. What more could we have wished for our consolation and peace in these difficult times than that the Vicar of Christ on earth himself in his own voice—and whoever hears it, hears Christ himself—has deigned to comfort us and spur us on to take upon ourselves the care of this rule of life that is ours and to love it? Now we must make sure that from this exceptional blessing of God we derive the most fertile fruit possible. In the first place, let us open our hearts before God, thanking the Father of mercy and the God of all consolation, who comforts us in all our tribulations. Let all be careful not to dishonor the divine blessing with any kind of arrogance, but rather to demonstrate to all a joy tempered by modesty, sobriety, and due humility.

2. Let all remember, then, how appropriate it is that those who make their profession in the Society should be in conformance with it. The purpose of the Institute is holy and pious, and holy and pious are the means it proposes to use in order to achieve this purpose, with the approval of the Vicar of Christ on earth. Therefore all our thoughts and our decisions turn to that purpose, and we consider that none of the means that are contained in our Constitutions should be overlooked. In this way all our actions and our life will be conformed to piety and holiness.

3. Furthermore, it is fitting and appropriate that our respect for the Holy Roman Apostolic See be demonstrated by our ready and devoted obedience and our extraordinary ardor. The authority conferred upon it by Christ and the particular rule of our Institute, as well as all the numerous and singular blessings we have received from it, require it. Indeed, if all of us obtain these fruits from this heavenly blessing, which I greatly hope, we will become worthy of new gifts of divine mercy.

4. Finally, since the Most Holy Pontiff Clement XIII has given us this solemn and public witness of his paternal benevolence and pity toward us as well as much more, it is fitting that we respond to this extraordinary blessing with the greatest possible demonstration of gratitude. Therefore, I ask Your Reverence to promulgate throughout the Province all these sentiments of mine. I ask too that you have each priest celebrate six Masses and that each brother recite an equal number of rosaries for the Supreme Pontiff, that God will long preserve for us and for the whole Church an excellent pastor

and father, grant him all good things, and with heavenly help assist and guide him in all his holy decisions. I also entrust myself to your prayers and ask you to remember me in your Masses.

Rome, January 16, 1765

Your servant in Christ

Lorenzo Ricci

Letter of M.R.P. Lorenzo Ricci to the Fathers and Brothers of the Society
June 17, 1769

It is necessary to pray with greater fervor because of the ever more serious dangers facing the Society

1. In past years, while we were oppressed by very serious misfortunes, I did not fail in my duty. Although overwhelmed by sorrow, I more than anyone needed someone to comfort me in the desolation of my soul, to urge me to endure with strength such adversity. I have never ceased to exhort you in every possible way to patience, to hope in the help of God our Lord in our difficulties through Jesus Christ and his most holy Mother, whom I designated in a special way as our intercessors, to pray for us before God. And in truth, neither my concern nor your prayers have been deprived of their desired fruits. The unflagging constancy and strength of mind, never weakened by any difficulty, never dimmed by any worry, with which our exiled brothers have endured so many great misfortunes not only with patience, earning the admiration of all, but also with joy, as the apostles once did, are for us proof of the principles by which they were governed in the midst of so much suffering; they were also proof of the way in which God was at their side to strengthen their patience. Yet God has not yet released us from our tribulations, either because we are not yet completely free from those sins to which with a humble and sincere heart we must attribute the cause of our ills or because,

pleased with our capacity for endurance, he has postponed to a more opportune moment our consolation.

2. Whatever the reason that God did not grant our requests completely, we must not waste our time seeking it, since that would be useless. We must bear his trials with serenity and await the time of his mercy with hope and patience. And we will certainly wait patiently if we remember that all our adversities happen to us by the most just will and decision of God, our most loving Father, who directs everything for our good and for his glory. And we will wait with hope if we remember that the most loving Father does not abandon his children who hope in him or reject their prayers. And now we must commit ourselves with even greater fervor, because to our past misfortunes, prolonged and painful, new and worse tribulations will be added. Dangers are approaching and loom large, not just for one part of the Society or another, but for the whole. Therefore our prayer rises "as incense" before God (Ps 141:2). May that prayer, springing from hearts contrite with sorrow and lit by the fire of charity, match in intensity the greatness of the danger and the depth of the love each one has for our blessed Mother.

3. And since all the devotions previously prescribed by me, on which we must insist until God has mercy on us, concern the reverence to be shown to the blessed Virgin and the Most Sacred Heart of Jesus, I would like you, when you are engaged in these devotions, to do so with all your soul and with the certain hope and confidence of obtaining what you ask for. The present danger will strengthen our efforts. Our faith and peace of the soul will increase if, when imploring the protection of the Virgin, we keep in mind that she is the

Mother of God and our mother. Since she is the Mother of God, she has supreme power to pray to her Son; and since she is our mother, it is inevitable that she will be deeply touched and moved by our misfortunes. In your daily visits to the Most Blessed Sacrament or on the feast of the Most Sacred Heart of Jesus, when you ask him to increase and renew your hope, I would like you to remember his immense love for us and above all the words with which, while he was alive among us, he opened his heart to us, gently inviting all who were fatigued or burdened by oppression to take refuge in him and find comfort in their misfortunes, saying: "Come to me, all you that are weary and are carrying heavy burdens, and I will give you rest" (Mt 11:28). Mindful of his promise, let us place before him the misfortunes that overwhelm us. The Heart of Jesus, spontaneously disposed to mercy, cannot but be moved by them. And if it seems that he does not hear our prayers, as if he is asleep—as sometimes happens to test our faith—let us not lose heart but cry out with even greater strength, trusting that we will obtain what we seek, as the psalm says: "Rouse yourself! Why do you sleep, O Lord? Rise up, come to our help" (Ps 43:23, 26), or like the apostles when, in grave danger because of a sudden storm, they implored him: "Lord, save us! We are perishing!" At these words, Jesus, who was with them on the boat but asleep, woke up and "rebuked the winds and the sea; and there was a dead calm" (Mt 8:25-26). Above all, we must prevent fear from weakening or crushing our hope, so as not to be rebuked like the apostles: "Why are you afraid, you of little faith?" (Mt 8:26). There is nothing that weakens the strength of our prayers more than little faith, which is like a dark cloud that our prayers cannot penetrate.

4. To the spiritual practices that I have already recommended, which I wish you to continue wholeheartedly in the future, this year I would like you to add another: that everyone gather for nine days before the feast of our holy father Ignatius to pray for at least half an hour. Let us all, prostrate at the feet of our esteemed father, pray to him from the depths of our hearts that, with God, he himself may watch over and protect his sons and the Society he founded to fight God's battles and increase his glory. To enhance the fervor of our prayers, we add to them the exercises of virtue and above all of mortification as appropriate, according to the desire of each one and the decisions of the superior. To move the heart of our holy founder toward us, during these nine days each of us should examine himself and with a sincere heart think about how to amend his life according to the form, the example, and the documents that he left us, in such a way that the our holy founder may find and recognize himself in us, through our imitation of him. Such a change will also be of benefit as a tacit but clear and convincing defense to which we can resort. At this time, more than at any other, "we have become a spectacle to the world, to angels and to mortals" (1 Cor 4:9). Everyone looks at us, everyone watches us carefully: friends, because in our life, inspired by the rule, they find a valid argument to defend us; enemies, because they are looking to find something for which they can put us to the test and reproach us. For this reason I urge you, with deep feeling and in the words of the Apostle, to "behave properly toward outsiders" (1 Thes 4:12). Let us not be satisfied with the interior virtue that makes us pleasing in the eyes of God, but let us commit ourselves to letting it shine and be made manifest also to the eyes of men, so that those who scrutinize us with an accusing eye—as alas too many do—may see us acting, dealing,

and speaking in a measured and modest way, as clothed with Christ, according to what the Apostle himself says; that those who are most alienated and hostile may be obliged to respect our works: "then any opponent will be put to shame, having nothing evil to say of us" (Ti 2:8). I urgently commend these tasks to all, and I expect everyone to perform them, in the name of the deep affection they have for the Society, which prefers to defend itself with sanctity of life rather than with speeches. Make these practices known to the houses in your province. I entrust myself to you particularly in the celebration of the Eucharist.

Rome, June 17, 1769

Your servant in Christ,

Lorenzo Ricci

LETTER OF M.R.P. LORENZO RICCI
TO THE FATHERS AND BROTHERS OF THE SOCIETY
February 22, 1773

*A new exhortation to pray
at a time of extreme danger for the Society*

1. The holy prophet David admonishes us to keep our eyes constantly turned to God in times of difficulty, until he, moved with compassion, comes to our aid: "Our eyes look to the Lord our God, until he has mercy upon us" (Ps 123:2). I trust, dearest Fathers and Brothers in the Lord, that you will persist in prayer with perseverance, as I have already asked of you on other occasions in the name of your love for the Society, which has long been in difficulty. Your love for the Society is such that you have no need to be encouraged to pray more; nevertheless, my sorrow demands that I once again ask that you do so.

2. Not without dismay I see that God has not yet deigned to raise his hand to our aid. He has certainly given us very many proofs of his love and benevolence toward us, and in many places we have experienced his presence and his particular and almost extraordinary protection; nevertheless, he allows free rein to our misfortunes. I trust that his judgments are always just; the cause of our misfortunes I attribute to our faults, and above all to mine, and I sincerely confess to him: "Since we have sinned... all that you have done to us, you have done it with right judgment, O Lord" (Dn 3:29, 31 Vg).

And yet, what? Perhaps our God, whose nature is goodness, will forget to exercise his mercy? "Has God forgotten to be gracious?" (Ps 76:10). We know well that he, even when he is angry, remembers his extraordinary mercy. We know that his acts of mercy are far more abundant than those of his justice and all his other attributes. Therefore I pray, and you pray with me, that he may remember our fragility and weakness, and that his heart may be moved toward mercy and pity. If he in his justice wishes to consider our sins, let us pray that he may look at them in the light of his Son Jesus, who took them upon himself and so overabundantly made satisfaction for them. Finally, let us pray for the gift of a contrite and humble heart, a heart that he himself will never despise or refuse. Our sins must not prevent us from trusting strongly that God will give glory to his holy name, acting in accordance with his infinite mercy. Still less must these frightening times weaken our confidence; indeed, if we consider them carefully, they must strengthen our confidence. We are completely alone and deprived of all human affection; therefore God has reserved for himself the taking care of us and he desires that we not turn to anyone for help if it is not pleasing to him. He acts toward us in a very loving way, teaching us that we must not trust in men or place our hope in others, but rather that we must give thanks only to him. Accordingly, the triumph of his mercy will be greater, because it will be clearer and more visible. What then shall we fear, if God is our shield and our defense? Indeed, it will be an advantage for us to be abandoned by men, since God has testified to wanting to be the father of orphans and the defense of the forsaken. In humility and trust, strong and sincere, we raise our hands and our eyes to heaven, to the Lord who prides himself on being called on for timely help in tribulations, imploring his help and his mercy.

3. But prayer must be fervent. In his psalms, which illustrate the practical discipline of prayer, the holy prophet David often shows us that he prays to the Lord from the depths of his tribulations, and not in a low voice, but with loud cries and clamorous lamentations. There are many examples of this, including: "Out of the depths I cry to you, O Lord" (Ps 130:1); "In my distress I cry to the Lord" (Ps 120:1). Such cries and lamentations indicate the fervent effort with which we must pray, an effort that is as great as the suffering we endure and as strong as our desire to obtain liberation from it. There is no need for me to expound on how many and how great are the afflictions the Society is enduring. Everyone knows that the present tribulations are extreme, and extreme is the fear of future ones. You want the Society to be liberated from these tribulations, with an intensity as great as the love you have for it. And rightly so. In fact, the Society has shown you the way of salvation; there can be for us no benefit greater than this or closer to our hearts.

4. Our prayers are made in the name of Jesus Christ. They must be so if they are going to be effective, capable of moving the heart of the Father. As Jesus himself said: "If you ask anything of the Father in my name, he will give it to you" (Jn 16:23). But who could doubt that our prayers are in the name of Jesus Christ? Asking in the name of Jesus, as Saint Augustine explains, means asking for what Jesus favors, for what leads to eternal salvation. For what do we ask as we pour out our prayers to God for the preservation of the Society and for our perseverance in the Society? Let us pray to God that he may allow us to persevere in that vocation through which we were called by him to this pious, holy, praiseworthy Order, which is so very fruitful, dedicated as it is to promoting the honor of

God and the salvation of souls, as the Church and vicars of Christ have declared. Let us pray that we may be allowed to accomplish with fidelity what we promised to God when we pronounced our holy vows; that our life might conform to those laws prescribed to us by our sainted father, who burned for the salvation of souls, enlightened by the light of God and by the divine will to write them, laws that draw on divine wisdom and are written in the light of the holy Gospel, as is evident to all who consider them carefully. Finally, let us pray that we may be able to follow in the footsteps of the many canonized saints as well as of the numerous men of extraordinary holiness who, through the faithful observance of these laws, reached the peak of perfection, amassed great merit, and now enjoy extraordinary happiness in heaven. What great hope must we have when we consider that our prayers are truly offered in the name of Jesus and that when we pray in his name there is nothing that is not granted.

5. In addition to these intrinsic aspects of prayer, there is an extrinsic aspect that is able to strengthen it and increase its effectiveness. How much strength is added to our prayer when it is accompanied by an innocent and sinless life and many acts of holy virtue? The requests made of a prince by men who are very pleasing to him are more generously received and what they ask for is more easily obtained; in like manner the prayers offered to God by innocent and holy souls who are very pleasing to him often result in great blessings—so much so that sometimes the laws of nature are loosened and miracles occur. This is why the more we advance in friendship with God, the more effective our prayers will be; the more willing the angels will be to bring them before the throne of God; and the saints whom we invoke as our patrons will with

greater passion join their prayers to ours. Saint Ignatius in particular, and all the others of the Society who are among the blessed in heaven and who now love even more deeply this Order that led them there, will, with the greatest solicitude, seek a favorable response to the prayers of the faithful members of the Society.

6. Therefore, dearest Fathers and Brothers, animate your prayers by approaching every exercise of piety carefully and fervently, with mutual charity, with obedience to those who are for you in the place of God, bearing the labors, the worries, the poverty, the offenses, the separation, and the solitude, acting with prudence and evangelical simplicity, with actions that serve as good examples and with pious speech. Let us ask God to keep the Society formed in this spirit. If it were to happen that we were deprived of it—God forbid!—it would not matter if the Society ceased to exist, since it would then be useless in achieving the purpose for which it was established. Those who neglected to arouse in themselves such a spirit, and even more, those who sought to extinguish it in others, introducing a contrary spirit of non-observance, dissent, contempt, and rebellion, would bring the certain ruin of the Society, with greatest damage to the divine honor, the salvation of their neighbor, and their own. But God forbid that one of these be among you.

7. Here you have, dearest Fathers and Brothers, my request and the sole reason for which I am writing to you. I ask you to pray in the name of the whole Order. In the name of the same Order I pray for you, for your well-being, for that which is closest to your heart and is most important to you. I have no intention of calling for new prayers; however, I urge that

the ones I have already prescribed be continued, especially daily prayer before the Most Blessed Sacrament, a practice I would like to see perpetuated in the Society. I leave to each individual the decision regarding additional prayers, which the present tribulations call for, and the charity with which each embraces the Society. Devotional practices also be prescribed by superiors for set times. It only remains for me to entrust myself to your holy sacrifices and your prayers.

Rome, February 22, 1773

Your servant in Christ,

Lorenzo Ricci

LETTER OF M.R.P. JAN ROOTHAAN
TO THE FATHERS AND BROTHERS OF THE SOCIETY
July 24, 1831

On tribulations and persecutions

1. Certainly I have no reason to doubt, dearest reverend Fathers and Brothers in Christ, that all those who are happy to be sons of the Society and of Saint Ignatius are not only disposed to gladly carry out the tasks of their vocation and undertake any effort in exercising them but also ready to endure with strength any adversity—even desiring it, through the inspiration of divine grace, and welcoming it with joy. Nevertheless, the times in which we live seem to require me to encourage those who are most faithful, to exhort those who are weaker, and finally to console everyone with the words of the Lord to the best of my ability. And here is something that our sainted father seems to have understood through divine inspiration from the earliest days of the Society, when the Lord, from the cross, promised that it would be good for him and for his companions that the Society never be without persecutions. We know that our father later wished this for the Society, asking God insistently for it. This family not only experienced persecutions, and not in modest measure, in times past but it is also experiencing them today, in abundance. I do not know if ever there have arisen in so many places and at the same time so much hatred and envy of the Society by so many malevolent persons, so many calumnies and offenses, so much pillaging and exile. A great many of our people have

experienced many of these difficulties in different places in the space of almost a single year. We know that such difficulties are great gifts of God. But faced with them, we cannot help wondering if they will end soon or if they are to continue. For this reason I have decided to exhort you at least by letter—not being able to speak to you in person—to listen to what the times ask of us and to respond in a manner worthy of our name and our vocation.

2. First of all, the situation certainly is worthy of our gratitude. I do not really see how anything else could move us more to embrace our vocation closely and with great affection and to thank the Divine Majesty for it, since that great goodness led us, perhaps unaware of what was being accomplished in us, to that Society which deserved to share so much in the extraordinary fate that Christ deigned to call blessedness. In fact, he said, "Blessed are you when people revile you and persecute you and utter all kinds of evil against you falsely on my account" (Mt 5:11); and again, "Blessed are you when people hate you, and when they exclude you, revile you, and defame you on account of the Son of Man" (Lk 6:22). Certainly, dearest reverend Fathers and Brothers in Christ, we see that those words of the Lord are fulfilled in this family of ours, and our souls are greatly consoled. Men really do insult us and persecute us and lie about us, speaking every kind of evil against us. The harassment we experience is at the same time a fruitful source of grace. God and our conscience testify to the fact that we do not profess a life dedicated to the misdeeds of which we are accused and which many who are ignorant believe; that we are in fact men and not monsters or freaks and causing ruin and plague for the State. Many discriminate against us, seeing us as lawless and wanting to deny

us the freedom and protection of the law which they advocate for the rest of humanity, as if we were criminals, considered guilty without evidence and convicted without cause. Finally, they would strip us of our name as if it were an evil, for no reason except for the fact that the Son of Man has deigned to call us to communion in his Name. And therefore they have declared war on this most holy Name. They hate this Name, and they demonstrate their hatred in words and deeds, both when they denounce us to those who hunt down piety and faith and when they exercise their detestation of us in the same way in which they openly persecute the Vicar of Christ and his holy Church and anything related to virtue, chastity, or Christian piety, being, as they are, hostile haters of the entire Church.

3. Therefore, the fact that we receive from the world the same hatred that our Lord Jesus experienced and that we have the noble calling to share in his cross is certainly a reason for gratitude, dearest Fathers and Brothers. Yet I admit that I cannot mention these things without bewilderment: Who am I, Lord, that you willed to have me share in so much and such great glory? And how is it that you consider me worthy of the fate of your dearest and most faithful servants? Certainly the Apostle Paul emphasized the divine blessing granted to those who had "the privilege not only of believing in Christ, but of suffering for him as well" (Phil 1:29). Peter, too, exhorts those who bear shame in the name of Christ to consider themselves blessed, because "the spirit of glory, which is the Spirit of God, is resting on [them]" (1 Pt 4:16, 14). Those who carefully consider the power of these words will understand that hardly even in heaven can anything greater be found, except for the beatific vision. The Lord did not want his strong ath-

letes to be deprived of rejoicing in hope (cf. Rom 12:12). He even says: "Happy are you when others insult you... rejoice and be glad, for your reward is great in heaven" (Mt 5:12). He allows some very fervent ones to experience joys already prepared and present even in the anguish of the cross, as in the case of one of them who said: "I am filled with consolation; I am overjoyed in all our affliction" (2 Cor 7:4).

4. And so this must be our first sentiment, dearest Fathers and Brothers in Christ, worthy companions of Jesus and sons of Ignatius, whenever we "face trials of any kind," that we "consider it nothing but joy" (Jas 1:2). And far be it from us that the vocation to the Society seem to anyone to be a blessing of lesser greatness for the fact that it is seen as a sign of contradiction. We must learn to value it all the more for this very reason, to consider it an even more extraordinary gift of God, and to guard it with greater passion. Certainly it is necessary to cry with bitter tears over the case of some few who, either because "when [they] noticed the strong wind, [they] became frightened" (Mt 14:30) or because they were not firm enough in God and not sufficiently "rooted and grounded in love" (Eph 3:17), were taken from us, and we groan for them, who put their hands to the plow and then turned back. May it be far from us to bring dishonor to our glory by doing harm, as Saint Bernard rightly said: "I believe a good life is one that performs many good deeds and endures many adversities, persevering in this way until the end."

5. But this inconstancy and sad ruin of those few whom I have now recalled suggests to us another consideration, which I strongly desire be aroused in all of us by the harassment we experience: that with a happy and steadfast mind for

the goodness of the cause, we join to holy solicitude also a true and profound humility. And indeed, nothing could be more glorious than to live our vocation—that is to say, to live a life of virtue, in the Church for the sake of Christ. Nevertheless, we can and must be aware that, if the world hates us in the same way that it hated God himself, it could happen that God may grant to the world the power to punish us for our faults—perhaps not all of our faults, but some of them. Even if these faults do not seem serious in the eyes of men, they are in the eyes of God, who is most pure and brighter than the sun, so that we merit all that we undergo, and even worse. In fact, dearest Fathers and Brothers, how can we rejoice, how can we be pleased with ourselves, how can we persuade ourselves that we are conformed to what our vocation requires? Perhaps there is one among us who seems to have done enough, who lives happily in a certain mediocrity of virtue. This would, as our sainted father said, be considered good and worthy of praise among men of the world; among us, however, it should be considered little or nothing. How can we compare it with what is required by our Order, our rule, our motto *"Ad maiorem Dei gloriam,"* the great name of "Society of Jesus" that we bear, and finally with the many and great blessings of God toward us? How much, I ask you, should rectitude and sincerity of intention be in all of us? How great should be our familiarity and union with God in prayer and actions? How much contempt should each of us have for his own name and his fame and for all worldliness? How much disregard for his own advantage? How much desire for and endurance of pain for Christ? How much readiness and perfection in obedience? How much abnegation of his own thoughts and his own will? How much purity of the apostolic and angelic life and purification even from the slightest faults? How much union and concord of charity between us? How much passion for the salvation of others? How much commitment? And finally, how much concern for responding to one's vocation and to fulfilling one's duty, not according to personal judgment, but following those laws that our predecessors wisely left us, on which alone a religious order stands and flourishes and earns more abundant divine assistance? And yet I confess to being often driven by the fear that God, due to the neglect perhaps of some, perhaps of a few, in achieving a solid and perfect virtue, sees that his Society needs not approval but rather purification. I fear, I say, that, just as "Satan has demanded to sift all of [us] like wheat" (Lk 22:31), so also God himself has decided to purify his threshing floor. And certainly his words are such as to awaken and rightly shake anyone who is lazy or asleep: "He removes every branch in me that bears no fruit. Every branch that bears fruit he prunes to make it bear more fruit" (Jn 15:2).

6. And so this is another sentiment that I want to be awakened in us by the misfortunes we suffer or that we rightly fear, that we "humble [ourselves] therefore under the mighty hand of God" (1 Pt 5:6). It certainly will be of no help, dearest Brothers and Fathers, if we delude ourselves and deceive ourselves, if we persuade ourselves that we can so easily, with little effort and, so to speak, so cheaply be true sons of Ignatius and true companions of Jesus. On the contrary, the sentiment of humility of which I speak is always very necessary. "The greater you are, he says, the more you must humble yourself; in such a way you will find grace before the Lord" (Sir 3:20 Vg). If we are truly humble, we will find grace from God, from whom alone it is sufficient to find grace, even if grace from men, which is fallacious in itself, diminishes or decreases. Therefore, considering the reason for our vocation, we ask the Lord this, with all possible humility: "Lord, let me know

my end...let me know how fleeting my life is" (Ps 38:5). Considering with care and from a heavenly perspective the purpose for which each one of us has been called and made not only a Christian but also a religious in the Society of Jesus, the purpose for which each of us has been placed in the office we hold, in the task for which we are responsible, we see how much we lack and we weep at our imperfection. We aquire new energy to remain firm in our commitment to following in the footsteps of our fathers and to the faithful imitation of Christ, who is our guide and living example. And therefore I feel that we must appease God with the humble solicitude of which I have spoken; with it, I trust that even the strength of our persecutions will finally be weakened and broken, so that, as the sage says, "When the ways of people please the Lord, he causes even their enemies to be at peace with them" (Prv 16:7). May the Lord enlighten their blind minds, touch their hearts, and from hostile enemies finally make them advocates of our work, thanks to which not only can we desire their good and pray for them but also do good according to our duty. For the rest, if we have this disposition of mind of which I have spoken, whatever happens, according to the will of God, we will experience the truth of that famous phrase made known by the Church: "No adversity will harm us, if no iniquity will dominate us."

7. Dearest reverend Fathers and Brothers in Christ, I would not like anyone's confidence to be the least bit diminished by what I have said about nurturing humble solicitude. I desire this and ask it because the more we are humble toward ourselves, the greater trust we will have in God. May we awaken humble solicitude in ourselves by virtue of divine grace and with the help of holy prayer and may we maintain it to the highest degree

possible. In fact, dearest Fathers and Brothers, if among you there are some who have been struck down by the fear of future evils, "Why," I ask, "are you afraid, you of little faith" (Mt 8:26)? "Does disaster befall a city, unless the LORD has done it" (Am 3:6)? But can what the Lord has done be an evil? And if not everything that the Lord allows is necessarily a good, is it not certain by faith that everything, even misfortunes, "work together for good for those who love God" (Rom 8:28)? And in truth, if we love God, what can he do to us that is evil? What is there that will not benefit us greatly?

8. In the face of our tribulations, of all the evils we fear may come, we ask: When will the fury of the whole world and also all of hell finally cease? Perhaps it will bring us to face violent hands, jail, wounds, threats of death? Certainly these would be extreme situations, the worst. And yet does God himself perhaps not say of these same situations, "Do not fear those who kill the body" (Mt 10:28)? I think, dearest Fathers and Brothers, and I do not doubt that you too will think, that giving one's life and shedding one's blood for a good cause is good—so much so that, if we expect something similar, even if we are frightened, perhaps we are being somewhat presumptuous, aspiring to such great glory of which we are completely unworthy. If only we were worthy of it! If only even a few of us were worthy of such a blessed fate! How many—I ask—among our fathers, apostolic men, were nourished solely by some hope of so great a good in their labors and concerns? They proposed for themselves this single goal as a reward that they did not achieve despite the hardships and worries of so many years. But if we feel we are unworthy of such a great good, at least, I ask you, let us not fear it. Rather let us remember that Christ, in describing the gravest threats of the world—

"You will be hated by all because of my name" (Lk 21:17)—concluded his words with that unexpected and extraordinary sentence: "But not a hair of your head will perish" (Lk 21:18). Certainly a great many of our people have experienced this in an extraordinary way, having emerged unscathed from dangers with the protection of divine providence.

9. What, then, shall we fear? Perhaps that, deprived of what until now divine providence has given us to live, returned to hardships and oppressed by poverty, we might end up lacking not only what is helpful but also what is necessary? While now we certainly live with ease and are sustained thanks to generous daily almsgiving, would that we might be worthy of tasting at times the very fertile fruit of holy poverty. We would become more like those fathers of ours who were rich in virtue, in heavenly gifts and merits before God, while being poor in their way of living. Their poverty was not something they simply aspired to; it was something they experienced, sometimes lacking even the necessities of life. For this reason, I gladly remind you of those words of our sainted father, which move me every time I read them: In fact, *since the first who gathered in the Society were tested by a similar poverty and by a very great shortage of what is necessary for the body, those who enter after them will have to make sure that they reach the same point, as far as possible, as they progress toward God* (*Exam. Gen* 4:26). It is worth remembering what the evangelist Luke reported about the Lord Jesus, who asked his disciples: "'When I sent you out without a purse, bag, or sandals, did you lack anything?' They said, 'No, not a thing'" (Lk 22:35).

10. But if death or deprivation are not to be feared, perhaps some other evil will come upon us, such that we will be sepa-

rated and dispersed because of the force of persecution. I do not deny, dearest Fathers and Brothers, that this would be for me, and no less also for you, the hardest test of all. Nonetheless, however, if God were to permit such a test, however hard, it would still be a test, not perdition. Does not "the earth...and all that is in it" belong to the Lord (Ps 24:1)? Wherever we may be, will we not always be children of that providence that does not know how to abandon what it loves because it is completely the love of a father? Finally, even if something similar were to happen, it would not last forever but only for a brief time, in which our virtue and our constancy would be put to the test. And if we happen to be dispersed, I have full confidence of heart that we will be reunited again, so much so that I will not hesitate to make the prophet's words my own: "This hope is placed in my heart" (Job 19:27 Vg). The great and frequent mercy of God, dearest Fathers and Brothers, that the Society has experienced so far in recent times, which causes even many outsiders to believe a sort of miracle has happened, does not allow us to doubt that he himself will want to complete the work he has begun. Therefore if he strikes us, he will heal us, if he disperses us, he will gather us. Let us strengthen our hearts, all of us, and whatever fate God has set for us, let us boast with the Apostle even "in our sufferings, knowing that suffering produces endurance, and endurance produces character, and character produces hope, and hope does not disappoint" (Rom 5:3–5).

11. The Society's boat is at the mercy of the waves; this is not surprising. What amazes us when Peter's boat was shaken by a terrible storm? Certainly, the night and the power of darkness loom. We may struggle rowing. In fact, by Pius VII we have been described as rowers: we can be brave and never

broken by any effort! We may struggle with the oars, I say, "for the wind [is] against [us]" (Mt 14:24). But let us not stop, dearest Fathers and Brothers. The light will finally shine, and Jesus will come to be beside his own whom he sees in difficulty. Walking on the sea, he will stride over the agitated waves with his divine footsteps. The wind will cease and there will be calm. Let us cry out then and pray: "Lord, save [us]!" (Mt 8:30). Yet we must not be too afraid to die, so as not to be reproached like the apostles as men of "little faith" (Mt 8:26) by our most benevolent Lord. "Wait for the Lord; be strong, and let your heart take courage; wait for the Lord!" (Ps 26:14). "In a very little while, the one who is coming will come and will not delay" (Heb 10:37). Let us not stop asking God, "who gives to all generously and ungrudgingly" (Jas 1:5), that he may give to each of us what the Apostle calls a heart "strengthened by grace" (Heb 13:9). Let us also keep in mind the admonition of Peter: "Let those suffering in accordance with God's will entrust themselves to a faithful Creator, while continuing to do good... And after you have suffered for a little while, the God of all grace, who has called you to his eternal glory in Christ, will himself restore, support, strengthen, and establish you. To him be the power forever and ever. Amen" (1 Pt 4:19; 5:10-11).

I entrust myself to all your most holy sacrifices and to your prayers, dearest reverend Fathers and Brothers, beloved in Christ.

Rome, July 24, 1831

Servant in Christ,

Jan Roothaan

Against the Spirit of Fury

Diego Fares, SJ

The "spirit of fury" pervades human history. Its form may change, but it is always the same dynamic: one of opposition against "the other." We see it first in the anger of Cain, when it drove him to kill his brother. And it continues to be unleashed in the fury of the dragon who, unable to kill the woman, a symbol of the Church, turns its anger against the "rest of her children" (cf. Gen 4:6; Rev 12:17). New forms of this spirit today include "bullying" and "media persecution."

In a recent homily at Casa Santa Marta, Pope Francis reflected on the mystery of evil that is revealed in bullying, in the act of "attacking the weakest." He noted that "psychologists might have other explanations for the strong abusing the weak... but even children can have this trace of original sin, the work of Satan."[1]

The fact that Pope Francis refers to Satan tells us something about the spiritual character of this attitude, which, according to some words we use to name it—*accanimento*[2] in Italian or

---

1. Pope Francis, Homily at Santa Marta, January 8, 2018.

2. Besides fury, the Italian word *accanimento* can also mean anger, fierceness, aggression, anger, excessive zeal, and ferocity.

encarnizamiento in Spanish—would lead us to think that it is something animalistic or carnal, but this is not entirely the case. Mixed and confused with this carnal dimension, there is a hidden addition of ferocity and of gratuitous cruelty which, when we see its effects, produces enormous discomfort and mental confusion. Consider, for example, the teenager driven to suicide because she cannot cope with the idea that a private image has been shared online and gone viral.

This spirit of fury is diabolical in the sense that it is against the law of nature: it is not only destructive but also self-destructive. It is contagious, and it produces negative effects at a social level: feelings of abandonment and discouragement, disorientation and confusion. Since it is hidden and often gets confused with other phenomena, there is a need to expose it to the light of spiritual discernment so that we do not fail in our search to find ways of resisting it. It is possible to succumb to the contagion of its perverse dynamism even while fighting against some of its effects.

We must also take into account the fact that, besides obviously destructive fury, there is another, more "polite" form, more subtle but involving equal and systematic cruelty.[3] Is it not perhaps symptomatic that we use the terms "inhuman" and "dehumanize" without sometimes thinking that we do not mean "animal" by them but rather something else?

A brief phenomenology of the spirit of fury will help us recognize it and better understand its malice, so that we can foster our desire to resist it with the help of the Spirit, reject

---

3. But there is also "another persecution of which we do not talk much," a persecution "disguised as culture, disguised as modernity, disguised as progress: it is a 'polite' persecution—I would say, a little ironically... The head of this *educated* persecution, Jesus named him: the prince of this world" (Pope Francis, Homily at Santa Marta, April 12, 2016).

it, and drive it out from our hearts and the social structures in which it is embodied. As the hymn Veni Creator says, *Hostem repellas longius* ("Drive the enemy far from us").

To understand how we can resist the spirit of fury without being infected, we will keep in mind a recommendation of Pope Francis given in his meeting with Jesuits in Peru, during his most recent apostolic trip to Latin America. On that occasion he referred to a little booklet, *Las cartas de la tribulación* ("Letters of Tribulation"),[4] saying that "these contain marvelous criteria of discernment, criteria of action so as not to allow ourselves to be dragged down by institutional desolation"[5] and "to find the path to follow... when the tempest of persecutions, tribulations, doubts and so forth, is raised by cultural and historical events... There are various temptations that mark this moment: challenging ideas, not paying attention to events, becoming fixated with the persecutors... dwelling on our own desolation."[6]

---

4. L. Ricci and J. Roothaan, *Las cartas de la tribulación* (Buenos Aires: Diego de Torres, 1988). At the beginning of 1987, after returning from Germany where he had worked on his doctoral dissertation on Romano Guardini, the then-Father Jorge Mario Bergoglio asked his Jesuit superior, Dan Obregón, a Latinist, to translate letters written to the Jesuits by two of their superiors general—Lorenzo Ricci and Jan Roothaan—in times when the Society of Jesus suffered persecutions (one of which was so fierce that it resulted in the suppression of the Order for forty-one years, from 1773 to 1814). The translated letters along with a preface written by Father Bergoglio were published as *Las cartas de la tribulación*. That preface, published online by *La Civiltà Cattolica* (hereafter *Civ. Catt.*) under the title "The Doctrine of Tribulation," is found in the present volume on pages 3–9.

5. Pope Francis, "Where Have Our People Been Creative? Conversations with Jesuits in Chile and Peru," in *Civ. Catt.* (February 2018).

6. Pope Francis, Encounter with the priests, religious, those in consecrated life, and seminarians. Santiago, Chile, January 16, 2018, at w2.vatican.va/. Cf. J. M. Bergoglio, "The Doctrine of Tribulation."

Among various temptations that arise in times of tribulation, we will highlight that of the "spirit of fury," through which the evil spirit tempts us not only to resist grace but to take a further step: it involves us and makes us become accomplices of his desire to destroy our own flesh.

The Phenomenology of Fury

Whenever we encounter fury, we react instinctively. Different languages refer to this phenomenon by emphasizing different aspects. In Italian, the term *accanimento* takes into account the subject—the *cane* (dog)—and highlghts the subjective aspect of fury. In Spanish, *encarnizamiento* refers to *carne* (flesh), emphasizing the object on which fury is exercised. English and French use "fury" and *ferocité*, respectively, highlighting the violence of the action itself. In German, *Hartnäckigkeit* means "stubbornness," underlining a physical trait that reveals a ruthless determination or unscrupulous pursuit of a goal.

If we analyze the phenomenon of bullying, for example, we see that it is not easily categorized, although certain recurring characteristics—premeditated aggression, a systematic nature, and asymmetry of power—allow us to put individual incidents in this category.[7] Nevertheless, the description of certain traits that are common in the abstract does not touch on the core of the phenomenon, its apparently unmotivated evil, which at some point intensifies exponentially and becomes contagious. This characteristics and others like it lead

---

7. Cf. G. Cucci, "Bullying and Cyberbullying: Two Phenomena on the Rrise," in *Civ. Catt.*, English ed. (March 2018): 34–47.

us to realize that this is not a merely instinctive and animal issue, but something more.

Contagion is a distinctive element to keep in mind when analyzing the spirit of fury. Not all of us experience the spirit of fury in the same way, but there is a common element: when we are faced with someone aggressive, it awakens a strong mimetic impulse to fury both in those associated with the aggressor and in those who defend the victim. When there is such fury, the seed of vengeance is planted, and over time the contagion spreads.

Another element that needs to be considered is that, while it may seem that human cruelty has always been the same and that with modern civilization certain things no longer happen, in reality the contrary is true: as technology becomes more sophisticated, the spirit of aggression becomes crueler in its daily effects and more politically correct in its modalites. Is it not symptomatic of this that we judge a remotely operated missile to be less ferocious than hand-to-hand fighting in a bloody melee? That we "see less blood" does not mean that the spirit of aggression has diminished; if anything, it has become more precise, more systematic, and even more inhumane.

Finally, here is a paradox. What encourages, sustains, and exacerbates fury is—at the same time—the weakness and resistance of the flesh. One cannot rage against something as solid as iron, or against something that offers no resistance, such as water or air. This paradox leads us to discover a contradiction. "Fury against flesh" is intrinsically senseless, since after a certain point it ceases being an adequate object for an excess of fury. At a certain point what comes naturally is the appeal to stop the aggression and to have pity. However, if there is anything that leads us to "put our fingers in our ears and attack again with renewed fury" a defenseless victim, it is the spirit of fury. This spirit is thus revealed as something that it is not merely instinctive, but the fruit of a lucid and free decision "to do evil for its own sake."

All this is to say, to discern, unequivocally, that it is correct to speak of a "spirit of fury" rather than an instinct. In reality, when we use expressions like "killer instinct" or "blood-thirsty animal," we project on the animal world a human cruelty, a cruelty actually chosen with a clarity and lucidity that the animal world does not have. And if there is cruelty in the animal world, it is limited by the rhythm dictated by impulse and the satisfaction of an instinct, something that occurs suddenly and is impossible to plan in advance.

When Fury Damages Dialogue

This leads us to analyze in a different way the phenomenon of "media persecution." If the spirit of fury remains confined to the world of words and violence does not become physical —but, at most, manifests itself in tone and gestures—this does not mean that we have left the sphere of aggression and find ourselves on a more civilized plane. Quite the opposite! It is precisely in violent words, lies, slander, defamation, detraction, and gossip that the spirit of fury dwells, and it prowls out from there.

Francis unmasks certain temptations clearly and drastically. Some scoffed—as if to say that the pope was exaggerating—at the fact that he told a group of cloistered nuns that if they gossiped, they were "terrorist sisters."[8]

---

8. Pope Francis, Homily during midday prayer with contemplative women religious, January 21, 2018.

Words, by their very dynamic, tend to become reality. Therefore it is important to understand that "to discuss aggressively" is a contradiction. Being fierce in dialogue is counterproductive. The essence of dialogue is not the words spoken or the speeches made, but the reciprocal approach of the interlocutors to a reality that requires explanation. When someone formulates a judgment, he or she proposes it for the other's consent, so as to be able to complement it by the other's point of view. If dialogue is nothing more than a façade behind which we have the objective of imposing our view or disdaining other people's views, then there is no dialogue. Fury is not a result of instinct but of logic—and the logic is that of the "father of lies" (Jn 8:44). It is confronted by a different logic, that of truth, as Jesus attested in the Gospel and the Holy Spirit discerns in every situation. The logic of the Incarnation is opposed to the logic of aggression.

Remedies against Fury in Las cartas de la tribulación

In *Las cartas de la tribulación*, mentioned above, Bergoglio finds some remedies to to help us in resisting this evil spirit without being infected. This is the so-called "doctrine of tribulation." The letters "constitute a treatise about tribulation and how to endure it."[9]

Celebrating Vespers in the Church of the Gesù in Rome on September 27, 2014, Pope Francis said: "While reading the letters of Fr. Ricci, one thing struck me: his ability not to be ensnared by these temptations and [rather] to propose to

---

9. J. M. Bergoglio, "The Doctrine of Tribulation." There are seven letters of Ricci and one of Roothaan.

the Jesuits, in times of tribulation, a vision of things that anchored them even more in the spirituality of the Society."[10]

For context, we add that the instruction on how to bear and resist temptation, as presented by Bergoglio in his short preface to *Las cartas*, is complemented by two other texts, forming a trilogy: one earlier, "La acusación de sí mismo,"[11] first published in 1984; and another, written in the first months after his transfer to the residence in Córdoba, titled "Silencio y palabra".[12]

First of all, it should be said that what is contained in *Las cartas* is not an abstract elaboration of spiritual criteria, but rather the source and fruit of an attitude that led an entire institution—the Society of Jesus—to accept its own suppression (which caused the death of many Jesuits) in obedience to the Church, without returning evil for evil.

This paradigmatic behavior in a "great persecution" gives us a spiritual context for confronting any other tribulation. It is in accord with the spirit of the First Letter of Peter, which tells us not to be surprised by the fiery ordeal of persecution (1 Peter 4:12).[13] This attitude mirrors the Letter to

---

10. Pope Francis, Celebration of Vespers and Te Deum in the Church of the Gesù, September 27, 2014.

11. Cf. J. M. Bergoglio, *Reflexiones espirituales* (Buenos Aires: Diego di Torres, 1987). The text "La acusación de sí mismo" contained therein had originally appeared in *Boletín de espiritualidad de la Provincia argentina de la Compañía de Jesús* 87 (1984). An Italian translation is available under the title *Umiltà: La strada verso Dio* (Bologna: EMI, 2013).

12. J. M. Bergoglio, "Ensañamiento," in *Reflexiones en esperanza* (Buenos Aires: Usal, 1992). The following references are to the Italian translation "Silenzio e Parola" (hereafter SeP) in *Non fatevi rubare la speranza* (Milan: Mondadori, 2013), 85–108.

13. Cf. Pope Francis, Press conference during the flight on the return from the apostolic visit to Chile and Peru, January 21, 2018.

the Hebrews, which recalls that we have not yet "in the struggle against sin, resisted to the point of shedding blood" (Heb 12:4).

In the spiritual paternity of those superiors general of the Society of Jesus, Bergoglio finds the most efficacious defense against the risk of falling victim to exaggerating persecutions. A paternal care of the wheat, without prematurely getting rid of the chaff, is the remedy that can "rescue the body from spiritual distress and rootlessness."[14] However, he does not suggest opposing an attack from the outside, but like a father, he helps his children "assume an attitude of discernment"[15] that allows them to defend themselves.

The most devastating effect of the spirit of fury attacking the weakest is seen in the faithful people of God: it falls upon those who are simple and childlike, those who, when they see this fury unleashed mainly against the defenseless and only mildly against the greatest, will experience abandonment, despair, and a sense of uprootedness. A paternal attitude consists in protecting the little ones from scandal. This was the first concern of Our Lord at the time of his passion : to pray to the Father so that his own would not be scandalized.

Humble Yourself to Resist Evil

The defenses against the spirit of fury do not involve trying to "defeat evil with evil," which by its nature results in contamination. On the contrary, they aim to strengthen our ability to resist evil by finding ways to endure tribulation

---

14. J. M. Bergoglio, *The Doctrine of Tribulation*.
15. Ibid.

without wavering. This type of resistance to evil is completely different from that other kind of resistance, against the Spirit, that the devil practices by provoking and instigating anger. Let us examine the characteristics of the first type.

In some cases, resistance to persecution will consist of a "flight into Egypt," mirroring what Joseph did to save the Child and his Mother: "We need to always have an 'Egypt' close at hand—even in our heart—to humble and empty ourselves before the exaggerations of someone who is suspicious of us"[16] and persecuting us. Therefore, the first option is to retreat, to not react by attacking or responding impulsively with direct opposition. Going to this place in our hearts, this place where we can always find exile whenever we are persecuted by a Herod, is the source of the peace the Lord gave to Bergoglio when he understood that he would be elected bishop of Rome. The pope himself has told the story many times, asking for prayers that he never lose this peace.[17]

However, in other cases the resistance would take the form of facing the evil spirit openly, giving public witness to the truth firmly but graciously. On this point, Pope Francis shows a special grace, which is—to put it plainly—that of "drawing out the evil spirit" who in this way reveals himself.[18] When temptation is based on a half-truth, it is very dif-

---

16. SeP 94. Romano Guardini indicates that this unbridledness (*Ausschweifen*) as characteristic of a person who is "dissolute, violent, corrupted by power and inner insecurity." (*Der Herr* [Würzburg: Werkbund, 1964), 22]).

17. Cf. A. Spadaro, "Interview with Pope Francis" in *Civ. Catt.* (September 2913): 450. Published in English as "A Big Heart Open to God: An Interview with Pope Francis" in *America* (September 30, 2013).

18. Cf. "Five years of Pope Francis: The Path of the Pontificate Gradually Unfolds," in *Civ. Catt.*, English ed. (April 2018): 1–8.

ficult to shed light and clarify things by intellectual means. "How can we be of help in such circumstances?" Bergoglio asked himself in *Silencio y parola*. "It is necessary to let the evil spirit show himself," and the only way to do that is make space for God, because Jesus is the only one who can force the devil to reveal himself: "There is only one way to make space for God, and this has been taught by Jesus himself: self-emtying, *kenosis* (Phil 2:5–11)—to be silent, to pray and to humble oneself."[19]

Bergoglio says, "We should focus on 'time' more than on 'light.' Let me explain: the light of the Devil is strong, but brief—like the flash of a camera—while the light of God is meek, humble, and unimposing—but it offers itself, and it is lasting. We need to know how to wait, praying and asking for the intervention of the Holy Spirit until the time of the strong light has passed."[20]

Political Dimension of the Fight against the Spirit of Fury

It is important to understand what is involved in the humbling of the self to make room for Jesus. It is not a simply a subjective religious attitude. In the dialogical process of "focusing on time," "acknowledging one's weakness," and accepting the real humiliation of not being able to explain everything, "another dimension" opens up.[21]

Our engagement in a type of dialogue that resists "the primordial cruelty inherent within us, which is rebellion

---

19. SeP, 102f.
20. SeP, 102.
21. Cf. SeP, 102.

against God," enables a political dimension of war, the "war of God," to become evident. Bergoglio uses the example given by a religious to describe this dimension: "Once, a religious, in referring to a particularly difficult situation, said, 'I understood that this was a war between God and the Devil. And if we humans decide to take up arms, we are destined for destruction.'"[22]

The awareness of this "political dimension" of the struggle against the spirit of fury is linked to the clarity with which Francis faces all conflicts—both those internal to the Church and those external to it. It is this awareness that it is God's war that makes him safe in peace, strengthens him in patience, and induces him to go out and go on.

Meekness Will Show Us to Be Even Weaker

As Austen Ivereigh wrote: "The Cross would eventually oblige the devil to reveal himself, because the devil mistakes gentleness for weakness."[23] Bergoglio affirms this: "In moments of darkness and great tribulation, when the 'tangles' and 'knots' cannot be undone, nor can things be clarified, then we must keep silent; the meekness of silence will show us to be even weaker, and then it will be the same Devil who, emboldening himself, will manifest himself clearly and show his true intention, no longer disguised as an angel of light but fully self-evident."[24]

---

22. SeP, 105.

23. A. Ivereigh, *The Great Reformer: Francis and the Making of a Radical Pope* (New York: Henry Holt, 2014).

24. SeP, 105.

This "showing ourselves to be even weaker" is the attitude that overcomes the insidiousness of the evil spirit. And it is the best approach against gossiping, scandalous remarks, and attacks that are easily spread through social media, even by publications calling themselves "Catholic." In such circumstances we must resist in silence. The reflections of Maximus the Confessor quoted by Bergoglio in *Silencio y parola* are interesting in this respect. They affirm that when Christ in his passion was becoming weaker—until his death on the Cross, alone, with his disciples fleeing—the devil seemed to gain in strength and became brazen, thinking himself victorious. But in the end it is the weakened body of Christ that becomes the bait the devil, in his fury, takes. And in this way he takes not only the bait but also the poison that neutralizes him.[25]

Some accuse Pope Francis of being confusing when he does not aggressively defend the righteous and condemn the sinners, impose rules, define with papal infallibility the lines we cannot cross, and so forth. But what they do not understand is that, in reality, whom he is actually confusing is the evil spirit that is motivating them.

In a world in which politicians and religious leaders debate and insult each other through tweets, Francis, with his way of resisting aggression through dialogue, "stands firm (Eph 6:13) but with the same attitude of Jesus,"[26] and opens around him a different political space, that of the Kingdom of God in which the real champion of the battle is not us, but the Lord.

---

25. Cf. Pope Francis, apostolic exhortation *Gaudete et Exsultate*, 115; SeP, 104.

26. SeP, 105.

This "passive resistance to evil"—which Bergoglio has always emphasized as the grace that belongs to the people, and upon which they patiently and wisely build their culture[27]—stands in opposition to, among other things, three attitudes that are typical of a "politics of aggression" and are at the basis of all partisan politics. Bergoglio describes these attitudes as they present themselves in the Passion of our Lord. The first one is the behavior of the people who "persecute those whom they believe to be weaker."[28] The powerful did not dare to oppose Jesus when the people followed him, but they were brave enough to do so when, after he was betrayed by one of his own, they saw him weakened. The second attitude is characterized this way: "At the root of all cruelty there is a need to unload one's own faults and limits ... and the mechanism of the scapegoat is repeated."[29] The third attitude belongs to those who, like Pilate, in the face of such fury decide to wash their hands of the matter and walk away.[30]

Self–accusation

In contrast, "showing oneself weak" in imitating Jesus consists of a very specific attitude. Bergoglio says that "Jesus forces the devil to 'show himself,' he makes room for this."[31]

---

27. Cf. D. Fares, "Io sono una missione: Verso il sinodo dei giovani," in *Civ. Catt.* (March 2018): 431.
28. SeP, 103.
29. SeP, 103f.
30. SeP, 104.
31. SeP, 105.

Of course, it is not possible for us to imitate what Christ obtains through his innocence and his unconditional self-gift into the hands of the Father for the salvation of all, even forgiving his enemies. But there is a way accessible to us sinners to make our own weakness innocent: it consists of the "accusation of self," an attitude diametrically opposed to one of fury toward others.

Self-accusation, not in a generalized sense, but in terms of something concrete, is to "show oneself as weak," so that we can be "defended by the Paraclete," in the same way that a defendant confides in and relies upon his lawyer to defend him most effectively in the face of his accusers. This idea was explored by Bergoglio in his commentary on Dorotheus of Gaza in the treatise "La acusacion de si mismo."[32] In fact, Dorotheus alludes to how good it is to shape one's own heart through the exercise of "self-accusation," since it concerns "interior attitudes," even small ones, that have repercussions at the institutional level."[33]

"It is not uncommon to find—in religious communities, be they local or provincial—factions struggling to impose a hegemony of their own thoughts and preferences. This happens when charitable openness to one's neighbor is replaced by personal ideologies. The whole of the family is no longer defended, just the part that concerns me. We no longer adhere to unity... but to conflict... He who accuses himself makes room for God's mercy."[34]

---

32. Cf. J. M. Bergoglio, *Umiltà: La strada verso Dio* (Bologna: EMI, 2013). The text reports and comments on a translation of "Instruction No. 7" from the spiritual teachings of Dorotheus of Gaza.

33. Bergoglio, *Umiltà*, 12.

34. Ibid., 11–12 and 27.

In his preface to *Las cartas* Bergoglio shows that bearing witness to the truth is something very different from merely "telling the truth." In the tribulation that leads to the suppression of the Society of Jesus, "it is not of God to defend truth at the price of charity, nor charity at the price of truth, nor equilibrium at the price of both of them. In order to avoid becoming a truthful destroyer or a charitable liar or a confused paralytic, one needs to discern."[35]

We must always be vigilant against this type of "fury"—especially when it manifests itself in an educated manner, even using the truth, because "Satan does not always tempt with lies. At the basis of a temptation there could in fact be a truth—although a truth lived out in a bad spirit, as Blessed Peter Faber [later proclaimed a saint] pointed out."[36] Bergoglio notes that an ideological truth must always be judged not for its content but for the spirit (the will) that sustains it, which is not always necessarily the Spirit of truth.[37]

As a remedy, a safer antidote to fury, Bergoglio supports the idea of "recourse to Jesuit sins" as made by the superiors general, sins that, seen from a merely discursive perspective rather than one of discernment—seem to have nothing to do with the external confusion caused by persecutions. "What happens is not a matter of chance: there is here a dialectic proper to the situational context of discernment—a dialectic that involves seeking interiorly within oneself a state of being similar to the external one. In this case, seeing oneself solely

---

35. Bergoglio, "The Doctrine of Tribulation."
36. Bergoglio, *Umiltà*, 85n11; cf. P. Faber, *Memoriale*, No. 51.
37. Bergoglio, *Umiltà*, 86.

as persecuted could engender the bad spirit of 'feeling like a victim,' like an object of injustice, for example. Outside, because of persecution, there is confusion... In considering his own sins the Jesuit asks for 'shame and confusion for himself.' This is not the same thing, but it seems so; and in this way he is better disposed to do discernment."[38]

Bergoglio notes that the superiors general "focus their reflection on the confusion" that the ideology underlying persecution produces "in the heart" (of the Jesuits, in this case). "Confusion dwells in the heart: it is the coming and going of different spirits."[39] And he continues: "Ideas are discussed, situations are discerned." The situation is one of confusion, and the cause of confusion is rooted in the dynamic of fury, that coming and going of thoughts that show up when one is under pressure from a fierce and persistent attack typical of those who are "stiff-necked."[40]

Resistance to the Holy Spirit, to his grace and the splendor of his truth, is that typically diabolic impetus which, in order to avoid looking at itself, unleashes itself in fury against the flesh of the other. Faced with this accusatory dynamism that has nothing to do with piety, the interior attitude needs to be—paradoxically—the accusation of oneself, sincerely and simply, without frills and without the fury of guilt: the accusation of self in the face of the mercy of God and of the community.

---

38. Bergoglio, "The Doctrine of Tribulation."
39. Ibid.
40. "You stiff-necked people..., you are forever opposing the Holy Spirit" (Acts 7:51): it is the accusation that Stephen addresses to those who, in response, will respond furiously against him.

A New "Letter of Tribulation"

A concrete example of this attitude was provided by Francis recently in a kind of new "Letter of Tribulation." He sent it on April 8, 2018, to the Chilean bishops after having read the report by Archbishop Charles J. Scicluna, who had listened "with heart and humility" to the testimonies of witnesses and victims of abuses committed by priests and bishops in that country. The spirit of the pope's letter, addressed to his brother bishops, is that of a father speaking to grown children who are themselves parents. This is the profound sense of the letter, which is also the spirit Bergoglio perceived behind the letters written by the superiors general of the Society.[41]

The paternal spirit is contrary to the spirit of fury. At the heart of Francis's fatherly concern are the victims and the country itself, Chile, which bleeds for the sins of the Church. The first tool of a spiritual father is discernment. The pope, as he writes to the bishops, wants "to humbly urge your collaboration and assistance in discerning the measures to be taken in the short, medium, and long term."

Francis invites the ecclesial community to put itself "in a state of prayer" with the aim of "repairing, as much as possible, the damage of the scandal and restoring justice." The evils the pope refers to have damaged our spirit and "cast us into the world weak, fearful, shielded in our comfortable 'winter palaces.'" They have produced "distress and rootlessness"[42] among the people of God. Therefore, to be able to re-

---
41. Bergoglio, "The Doctrine of Tribulation."
42. Ibid.

store and heal the wounds we should first of all accept being forgiven and consoled by God.

When desolation is so deep, the radical attitude we must take is, as we said, to accuse and humble ourselves—which is what Francis here is the first to do, without unloading blame onto a scapegoat, as many have tried to do, but taking it upon himself. In fact, he writes: "With regard to myself, I recognize, and I would like you to convey this faithfully, that I have made serious errors in the assessment and perception of the situation, in particular through the lack of reliable and balanced information. I now beg the forgiveness of all those whom I have offended and I hope to be able to do so personally, in the coming weeks, in the meetings that I will have with representatives of the people interviewed."[43]

These are the attitudes that can allow wounds to heal, wounds suffered by society because of evil and sin. These are the attitudes that can strengthen our belonging to Christ and to the body of the Church.[44]

---

43. Pope Francis, "Letter to the Bishops of Chile" following the report delivered by Archbishop Charles J. Scicluna," April 8, 2018.

44. Bergoglio, "The Doctrine of Tribulation."

II

The Tribulations of Today

The Beginning of Day

POPE FRANCIS

"The open wound of sex abuse"

FOUR LETTERS
TO THE CHURCH OF CHILE

Guide to Reading the Letters to the Church of Chile

Diego Fares, SJ

"An open, painful, and complex wound that has been bleeding for a long time"... This image, with which Pope Francis opens his "Letter to the Bishops of Chile" of May 15, 2018, is an apt description of the abuse scandal that has impacted both society and the Church in Chile. We will try to give an account here of Pope Francis's efforts to heal this wound. Given that those efforts are part of an ongoing process, we will offer a chronology of the most relevant facts and the steps taken. We will then reflect on the criteria of discernment that the pope has used to illuminate this reality in which "we are all involved," as he wrote to the country's bishops.

A significant moment, which seems to encapsulate many others and which in some way triggered the entire process, took place on January 18, 2018, when a journalist asked Pope Francis about the case of Bishop Juan Barros, the bishop of Osorno, Chile, who had been criticized for covering up sexual misconduct by clergy. The pope responded to her, "The day they bring me proof against Bishop Barros, I'll speak. There is not one shred of proof against him. It's all calumny."[1]

Three days later, on the pope's return flight from Peru to Rome, the usual press conference had a singular character. The testimony of various journalists who were present confirms that the pope invited journalists to ask any question they wished. It was in this context that the pope asked for forgiveness twice for his use of the word *proof* in his comments about Bishop Barros: "Here I must apologize, because the word *proof* caused so much pain for so many victims of abuse."[2] Several details in the pope's extended comments suggested that he had been following the case of the victims and the accused for some time.[3]

In these comments, which prompted many interpretations and are notable for the way the pope asked for forgiveness in the first person, we see the same attitude that Fr. Bergoglio described in 1987 as one that is "proper to the situational con-

---

1. Summer Meza, "Pope Francis Says Sex Abuse Victims Are Slandering Catholic Bishop They Say Helped Commit Sex Crimes," *Newsweek*, January 19, 2018. Available at https://www.newsweek.com/pope-francis-chilean-sex-abuse-victims-slander-against-bishop-785386.

2. Pope Francis, "Press Conference on the Return Flight from Lima to Rome," January 21, 2018. Available at http://www.vatican.va/content/francesco/en/speeches/2018/january/documents/papa-francesco_20180121_peru-voloritorno.html.

3. One fact was that the pope receives and listens to victims of abuse practically every week. Another was that Bishop Barros had twice submitted his resignation, and the pope had rejected it, saying that resigning because of external pressure meant admitting previous guilt and that, "in any case, if there is guilt, there is an investigation."

text of discernment—a dialectic that invoves seeking interiorly within oneself a state of being similar to the external state . . . and in this way [one] is better disposed to do discernment."[4] The pope acknowledged his fault and asked for forgiveness for something concrete that had hurt others. Having dones this, he was better able, as we will illustrate, to discern the next steps more clearly.

After a month of prayer and consultations, on February 19, 2018, Francis sent Archbishop Charles Scicluna to Chile with the task of listening humbly and with an open heart to victims and then preparing a report that would offer as independent a diagnosis and as clear a picture of the situation as possible. As the pope later wrote in his "Letter to the Pilgrim People of God in Chile," "the visit of Archbishop Scicluna and Monsignor Bertomeu resulted from the realization that there were situations that we did not know how to see and hear."[5]

After reading the report that was delivered to him on March 20, Francis took three steps. The first was "to meet personally with some of the victims of sexual abuse, the abuse of power, and the abuse of conscience, to listen to them and to ask forgiveness for our sins and omissions."[6] With regard to these meetings, it is important to note both the statements of the victims on what it meant for them to be together with the pope, and, for the Holy Father, the joy and hope that he

---

4. Jorge Mario Bergoglio, SJ, "The Doctrine of Tribulation," *La Civiltà Cattolica*, English ed., May 3, 2018. See pages 3–9 in this book.

5. Pope Francis, "Letter to the Pilgrim People of God in Chile" (May 31, 2018), n. 3. See pages 129–40.

6. Ibid.

derived from the fact that the victims spoke of many people who had helped them.[7]

On April 8 Francis took the next step. He summoned the Chilean bishops to Rome.[8] While they were gathered for their 115th plenary assembly in Chile, they received a letter from the pope asking them to meet with him, saying, "[I] humbly request your cooperation and assistance in discerning the measures that must be adopted in the short, medium, and long term in order to restore ecclesial communion in Chile, remedy the scandal to the extent possible, and re-establish justice."[9]

The meeting in Rome with the pope was held from May 15 to 17. At 4 PM on May 15, the pope met in the study of the Paul VI Auditorium with the thirty-four bishops who had come from Chile. After having offered a meditation, he gave each of them a ten-page letter[10] emphasizing several salient points, and he invited them to dedicate their time until their next meeting the following afternoon, May 16, exclusively to meditation.

---

7. Ibid., n. 6.

8. Pope Francis, "Letter to the Bishops of Chile" (April 8, 2018). See pages 109–12 in this book.

9. Ibid. Msgr. Bertomeu, who accompanied Msgr. Scicluna on his mission, highlighted the importance of this exceptional convocation of an entire episcopate by the pope, not only for the Church in Chile but for the universal Church. Cf. "Bertomeu sobre encuentro del Papa con obispos: 'Estamos haciendo historia,'" *Soy Chile* (May 17, 2018). Available at https://www.soychile.cl/Santiago/Internacional/2018/05/17/533919/Bertomeu-sobre-encuentro-del-Papa-con-obispos-Estamos-haciendo-historia.aspx.

10. Pope Francis, "Letter to the Bishops of Chile" (May 15, 2018). See pages 113–27 in this book.

On Thursday, May 17, there were two additional meetings during which the pope listened to the bishops, each of whom offered comments as his own prayer had suggested. That same day the pope presented the bishops with a letter in which he expressed his gratitude for their for their particiation in these meetings.[11]

On May 18, in a gesture of openness to the will of the pope, all the Chilean bishops offered him their resignations.[12] On May 31, Francis sent a letter to all the people of God in Chile.[13] On June 11, he accepted the resignations of Bishop Barros and of two other bishops,[14] and the next day he sent Archbishop Scicluna to Chile for a new eight-day mission aimed at conveying the pope's closeness to the people of Osorno and providing concrete technical and juridical advice to the diocesan administrations of Chile.

At the Mass celebrated in Osorno on Sunday, June 17, Archbishop Scicluna, kneeling and accompanied by the new apostolic administrator, Bishop Jorge Concha, said to the

---

11. Pope Francis, "Letter to the Bishops of Chile" (May 17, 2018). See page 128 this book.

12. "Declaración de renuncia de los obispos de Chile" (the text of the statement of the Chilean bishops after their meeting with the pope). Available at https://es.zenit.org/articles/ultima-hora-todos-los-obispos-de-chile-renuncian/.

13. Pope Francis, "Letter to the Pilgrim People of God in Chile."

14. These were Cristián Caro, the bishop of Puerto Montt, and Gonzalo Duarte, the bishop of Valparaíso, both of whom had reached their canonical age limits. Subsequently, on June 28, the pope accepted the resignation of two other Chilean bishops, Alejandro Goi Karmeli, the bishop of Rancagua, who had also reached the canonical age limit, and Horacio del Carmen Valenzuela Abarco, the bishop of Talca.

congregation: "Pope Francis asked me to seek forgiveness from the faithful of the diocese of Osorno and from all the inhabitants of this territory for having offended and deeply wounded them."[15]

While this process was going on—a process that would continue in the short, medium, and long term—the apostolic exhortation *Gaudete et Exsultate* was published. It was signed on March 19, the feast of St. Joseph, and officially presented on April 9.

It is not yet time to draw conclusions about a process that is still in progress. However, it may be beneficial to reflect on this new way of walking together and of interpreting reality that the pope is promoting among all the faithful people of God.

A Letter of Convocation: A Conviction, a Clarity, and a Hope

The first letter, dated April 8, summoning the Chilean bishops to Rome, is a call to conversion. The pope shares with his brother bishops *a conviction, a clarity*, and *a hope*: "the conviction that the present difficulties are also an opportunity to re-establish trust in the Church, trust shattered by our errors and sins"; the clarity that "without faith and without prayer, fraternity is impossible"; and the hope that "each of you may accompany me on the inner journey that I have been under-

---

15. Camila Mardones, "Charles Scicluna pide perdón de rodillas en nombre del Papa," *La Tercera* (June 17, 2018). Available at www.latercera.com/nacional/noticia/charles-scicluna-pide-perdon-rodillas-nombre-del-papa/210120.

taking in recent weeks," asking the Spirit to guide the process.[16]

We see that the pope puts first the task of restoring trust in the Church, and he therefore speaks of the necessity of conversion from sin and the healing of wounds. In this we see his discernment regarding the gravity of this type of sin. It is a sin in which the one who ought to protect others—that is, the consecrated person—has become one who abuses; it corrupts the hierarchical Church, which is called to be pure; and it produces "spiritual helplessness and rootlessness"[17] in the people of God. So the task is delicate: it is a matter of healing the Church and its pastors as well as the victims.

Francis proposes three means to accomplish this: self-accusation,[18] a paternal attitude toward one's brothers who are also spiritual fathers themselves,[19] and situating oneself in the bosom of the faithful People of God as a sound theological foundation from which all healing can begin.

---

16. Pope Francis, "Letter to the Bishops of Chile" (April 8, 2018).

17. Bergoglio, "The Doctrine of Tribulation."

18. The pope leads the way in this letter with accusation of himself that is not open to appeal: "With regard to myself, I recognize, and I would like you to convey this faithfully, that I have made serious errors in the assessment and perception of the situation, in particular through the lack of reliable and balanced information. I now beg the forgiveness of all those whom I have offended and I hope to be able to do so personally, in the coming weeks, in the meetings that I will have with representatives of the people interviewed."

19. This is the "profound meaning" of the letter, which is also the same spirit that Bergoglio perceived as having inspired the letters of tribulation of the superiors general of the Society. This spirit of fatherhood is opposed to the "spirit of fury."

Here the pope is not asking the bishops merely to invite the people of God in general to prayer; he is asking for listening "from the heart and with humility" to this preferential portion of the people of God: the victims and those who were of help to them.[20] While he was in Chile Archbishop Scicluna had collected sixty-four testimonials from victims of grave sexual abuse and abuse of conscience and of power by several consecrated persons.[21]

A Letter for Discernment in the Context of Prophecy and Synodality

The second letter, dated May 15, 2018, is the meditation that Pope Francis provided to the Chilean bishops and entrusted to their prayer for an entire day. This is the most significant letter of the set, since it expresses what is essentially the "interior journey" that the pope has traveled. It is significant that in this text he specifies concrete sins clearly and without euphemisms, and that he does so in several footnotes.[22] The actual people responsible for these sins and

---

20. Pope Francis, "Letter to the Bishops of Chile" (April 8, 2018).

21. Thus one can see in action the criteria of discernment on which Bergoglio reflected while reading the letters that the Jesuit superiors general wrote to the members of the Society in times of tribulation. See Diego Fares, "Against the Spirit of Fury," *La Civiltà Cattolica* (June 2018): 221–30; the text is included in this volume on pages 67–85.

22. In footnotes 22, 23, 24, and 25, the pope names each sin in no uncertain terms: abuse that is not only sexual in nature but also related to authority and power; divisions and the fractures in ecclesial community, cultivated since the seminary, along with making the

crimes must be condemned and punished, says the pope, but this in itself is not enough. In order to be able to discern the root of these sins, a "background of prophecy" and an "atmosphere of collegiality" are needed. He offers as the prophetic context of his meditation—key to grasping an adequate perspective of the problem[23]—the passage in which John the Baptist says, "He must increase, but I must decrease" (John 3:30).

Fundamental to the task of discernment for which the pope calls is the realizaiton that the temptation of "moving the problem onto the shoulders of others" must be avoided (Francis cites the episode of Jonah thrown overboard from the boat to calm the storm; cf. Gen 1:4–16). We must not give in to the temptations to ignore the root of the problem or refuse to get involved in it.

---

faithful participants in such divisions; entrusting diocesan or parish assignments that involve daily and direct contact with minors to religious expelled from their orders because of the immorality of their conduct; ways in which complaints are received, and ways in which they are minimized; failure to conduct or dilatory investigations into facts in the public domain, with the consequent scandal; pressure exerted on those who are to lead the trials; the destruction of compromising documents by those in charge of ecclesiastical archives; entrusting educational institutions for seminarians to priests suspected of active homosexuality.

23. The pope notes that the medicine used to alleviate the wound of abuse, "rather than healing it, seems to have made it even deeper and more painful." In his preface to the *Cartas de la tribulación*, Bergoglio pointed out that in their letters the main concern of the superiors general, faced with the tribulation experienced by the Jesuits and by those who took part in their apostolic works, was to focus on the problem: "It would appear that they feared the problem would not be properly approached" (Bergoglio, "The Doctrine of Tribulation").

Pope Francis reminds the pastors of how well the Chilean Church, throughout its history, has received the grace of being a prophetic Church and what it has been capable of on the occasions when this was called for. Indeed, it was able to proclaim the Gospel, to celebrate, to generate saints, to create vital spaces for the humblest peoples, to denounce violations of human rights during the Pinochet dictatorship. And all this fruitfulness was marked by the tenderness of Saint Teresa of the Andes, the joy of the faithful people in their expressions of popular piety, the prophetic gaze of Saint Albert Hurtado, the accompaniment of the Mapuche by the bishops of the south of Chile, the courage of Msgr. Silva Henríquez.

Francis concludes that "the holy and patient faithful People of God, supported and given life by the Holy Spirit, make visible the best face of the prophetic Church that knows how to put its Lord at the center in daily self-giving."[24]

After this exercise of historical memory, the pope turns to the sin of abuse, but—as noted above—not as a mere concrete matter that can be punished as a crime and/or forgiven in confession. He makes a discernment regarding the root of the sin: "It would be irresponsible of us *not to go deeper* in seeking the roots and structures that have allowed these concrete events to happen and perpetuate themselves."

His discernment leads the pope to conclude that the Chilean Church has lost its prophetic inspiration and made itself the center of attention. Instead of looking to Christ as the center, it focused on itself: "It stopped looking and pointing

---

24. Cf. Pope Francis, Apostolic Exhortation *Gaudete et Exsultate* (March 19, 2018), n. 9.

to the Lord in order to look at itself and take care of itself. It concentrated its attention on itself and lost the memory of its origin and its mission. It has focused on itself to such an extent that the consequences of this process have cost a very high price: *its sin has become the center of attention*" (the italics are the Pope's).

At this point, Francis introduces the basic criterion for this discernment, a criterion that opposes the "elite psychology" that has prevailed among a significant part of the Chilean clergy: the criterion of the whole and the part, and the place that the hierarchy occupies in the complex of the faithful people of God. "Awareness of the limitation and the partialness of our place within the people of God saves us from the temptation and the pretension of wanting to occupy all spaces, and especially a place that is not ours: that of the Lord."

It is significant that the word *synodality* emerges at the end of the letter, where the pope rejects the "scapegoat" mechanism in favor of a co-responsibility to "confess our weakness communally" in solving a problem that can truly be solved only if we "take it on collegially, in communion, in synodality"—a synodality that confesses common sin, a synodality that has been filled with mercy and converted into prophecy by vocation.[25] Against this prophetic and synodal background, the pope concludes, "Brothers, ideas are discussed, situations are discerned. We are gathered to discern, not to discuss."

---

25. Cf. Pope Francis, "Meeting with priests, consecrated men and women, and seminarians" (January 16, 2018). Available at http://www.vatican.va/content/francesco/en/speeches/2018/january/documents/papa-francesco_20180116_cile-santiago-religiosi.html.

A Letter of Thanksgiving and Sending Declaration of the Bishops

Together with the declaration of the Chilean bishops, who each offered their resignations to the pope, the letter that Francis addressed to the bishops at the end of the meetings[26] was published. In it, the pope *thanks them* for having accepted the invitation to make "a frank discernment" together in order to "collaborate" on the measures that will be taken; he *points out* again the gravity of the facts; he *emphasizes* that the bishops have united "in a single will and with the firm intention of repairing the damages caused"; and he *sends* them "to continue building a prophetic Church, one that knows how to restore to the center what is important: service to your Lord in the hungry, in the prisoner, in the migrant, and in the abused."

The Chilean bishops, placing "their assignments in the hands of the pope, so that he may freely decide regarding each one of them,"[27] have made "a collegial gesture—not without pain—to assume responsibility for the serious events that have occurred and so that the Holy Father may freely do with each of us as he chooses."[28]

---

26. Pope Francis, "Letter to the Bishops of Chile" (May 17, 2018).

27. "Declaración de renuncia de los obispos de Chile" (see note 12).

28. Ibid.

A Letter of Appeal to the Faithful People of God

At the beginning and end of the pope's "Letter to the Pilgrim People of God in Chile," released on May 31, 2018, Francis says his appeal, or the call, as he writes in *Gaudete et exsultate*, to the people of God is not an act of office, nor is it a mere gesture of goodwill; on the contrary, he wants "to frame things in their precise and meaningful place and put the issue where it ought to be." Citing the Second Vatican Council's Constitution on the Church *Lumen Gentium* (n. 9), the pope notes that this precise and valuable theological place is "the dignity and freedom of the sons of God, in whose hearts the Holy Spirit dwells as in His temple."[29]

"My appeal to you," the Pope writes, "is to invoke the anointing which as the People of God you possess."[30] Francis asks the faithful in Chile not to let themselves be robbed of that anointing and not to be afraid of being protagonists: "With you the necessary steps for ecclesial renewal and conversion can be taken."[31] He urges them to be creative and to say what they feel and think, always placing Jesus Christ at the center.[32]

The anointing of the Spirit that the pope invokes imprints a character on the people of God. It gives them a dynamic identity that makes them inclusive. It is the theology of the people of God presented in *Lumen Gentium*, and the

---

29. Pope Francis, "Letter to the Pilgrim People of God in Chile," n. 1.
30. Ibid., n. 7.
31. Ibid.
32. Cf. Ibid., n. 1.

Catechism reflects it when it teaches, "The People of God is marked by characteristics that clearly distinguish it from all other religious, ethnic, political, or cultural groups found in history."[33] At the same time, this identity causes it to "seek for the return of all humanity and all its goods, under Christ the Head in the unity of his Spirit."[34] And so, when the pope speaks of the people of God, he speaks inclusively of both the sheep and the shepherds, and of a people open to all peoples.

In this dynamic—"the life and history of a people" into which "God wanted to enter,"[35] as Francis says in *Gaudete et exsultate*—the anointing of God's people must find "concrete mediations to express itself." He exhorts the people of God to have "the courage to tell us [the pastors] 'I like this,' 'this is the way I think we should go,' 'that's not going to work.' ... Tell us what you feel and think."[36] And he urges the shepherds to learn to listen, because the people's questions, their pains, their battles, their dreams, their struggles, and their worries all have a hermeneutic value.[37]

When the pope speaks of the infallibility *in credendo* of the faithful people of God, he refers not so much to the technical formulations of the faith, but to the groans of the Spirit

---

33. *Catechism of the Catholic Church* (CCC), 782.

34. CCC 831, quoting LG 13.

35. *Gaudete et Exsultate*, n. 6. It is "a sacramental character or 'seal'" that "remains forever in the Christian as a positive disposition for grace, a promise and guarantee of divine protection, and as a vocation to divine worship and to the service of the Church" (CCC 1121).

36. Pope Francis, "Letter to the Pilgrim People of God in Chile," n. 1.

37. Cf. *Gaudete et Exsultate*, n. 44.

in the depths of the victims who bear the cross of the most vulnerable among the faithful people of God. It is the "thirst for God that only the simple and poor can know"[38] that the pope wants to highlight.

Starting from the recognition of the victims themselves of the presence of God through the good people who have helped them, as it were, in secret, the healing of the wounds that others have caused by abusing in secret can begin. The guiding criterion of this holiness is found in the Beatitudes, beginning with people who "know how to weep with those who weep, who hunger and thirst for justice, who look and act with mercy."[39] This is the perspective that shapes the structure of the entire apostolic exhortation *Gaudete et exsultate* on the universal call to holiness.

A New Practice and a New Hermeneutic

By considering the journey that the pope, the faithful pilgrim people of God in Chile, and its pastors are taking, we can draw some conclusions about the reality of the Church in which we are called to take part. According to the pope, we are offered an invitation to get involved, to walk in search of and to build among all a Church that is prophetic and synodal, a Church that is open to hope.[40]

---

38. Pope Paul VI, Apostolic Exhortation *Evangelii Nuntiandi* (December 8, 1975), n. 48.

39. Cf. Pope Francis, "Letter to the Pilgrim People of God in Chile," n. 6. Cf. *Gaudete et Exsultate*, nn. 76, 79, 82.

40. Cf. Pope Francis, "Letter to the Bishops of Chile" (April 8, 2018), Introduction and Conclusion; "Letter to the Bishops of Chile"

The prophetic character of this Church develops first of all in the "daily silence" of the people of God, "the entire body of the faithful that has the anointing of the Holy One,"[41] and testifies with "stubborn" hope that the Lord will not abandon us in suffering. "In this faithful and silent people," Francis states, "resides the immune system of the Church."[42]

The anointing of the Spirit, who "blows where and how he wills,"[43] promotes a new practice and a new hermeneutic from which flows a new way of reflecting theologically without "getting caught up in empty word games, in sophisticated diagnoses, or in vain gestures that would prevent us from having the courage to look directly at the pain that has been caused, the face of its victims, and the magnitude of what has taken place."[44]

The new practice is a movement "in a new direction,"[45] guided by the Spirit: without ignoring the pain; acknowledging conflict; listening—for those who do not listen impede progress; recognizing limits—otherwise one cannot advance; moving toward a culture of care and protection together with all those who make up our social reality—and recognizing the strength of the Spirit acting and working in so many lives. Without this movement, says the pope, we would "be taking only halfway measures, operating from a position that, far

---

(May 17, 2018), Conclusion; "Letter to the Pilgrim People of God in Chile" (May 31, 2018), Introduction and n. 7.

41. "Letter to the Bishops of Chile" (May 15, 2018).

42. Ibid.

43. Cf. Pope Francis, "Letter to the Pilgrim People of God in Chile," Introduction, nn. 1, 2, 5, 6.

44. Ibid., Introduction.

45. Cf. Ibid., n. 2.

from empowering what is good and remedying what is wrong, would minimize the reality, leading to grave injustice."[46] It is movement in a direction that is therefore more synodal, in the deepest sense of the word.

The new hermeneutic takes seriously the principle of incarnation and is aware that "doctrine, or better, our understanding and expression of it, 'is not a closed system, deprived of dynamics capable of bringing up questions, doubts, questionings,' since the questions of our people, their anxieties, their fights, their dreams, their struggles, possess a hermeneutical value that we cannot ignore,"[47] if we do not want to build lifeless structures.[48]

"To be 'the Church that goes out,'" writes the pope, is also to be a Church that allows itself to be "helped and challenged,"[49] including by the Spirit who blows where he wills. Thus, this new direction generates a new way of seeing. And, Francis adds, "neither an individual nor an enlightened group can ever claim to be the totality of God's people, let alone believe themselves to be the authentic voice of its interpretation. Thus, we must guard against what I allow myself to call 'elite psychology,' which can appear in our way of dealing with questions."[50]

Far from such "elite psychology," the pope shares what he learned as a pastor: "I learned that pastoral ministry of popular devotion is one of the few places where the People of

---

46. Ibid., n. 6.
47. Ibid., n. 5 (emphasis mine).
48. Cf. Ibid., n. 1.
49. Ibid., n. 5.
50. Pope Francis, "Letter to the Bishops of Chile" (May 15, 2018).

God is free from the influence of that clericalism that seeks to always control and block God's anointing of his people." Such devotion "is an invaluable treasure and authentic school where we can learn to listen to the heart our people and, at the same time, the heart of God."[51]

---

51. Pope Francis, "Letter to the Pilgrim People of God in Chile," n. 5.

Letter to the Bishops of Chile
April 8, 2018

Dear Bishops of Chile, Dear Brothers in the Episcopate,

The receipt last week of the latest documents that complete the report consigned to me by my two special envoys to Chile on March 20, 2018, totaling more than twenty-three hundred pages, has moved me to write this letter. I assure you of my prayers and I would like to share with you the conviction that the present difficulties are also an opportunity to re-establish trust in the Church, trust shattered by our errors and sins, and to heal some of the wounds that continue to bleed in the whole of Chilean society.

Without faith and without prayer, fraternity is impossible. Therefore, on this Second Sunday of Easter, on the day of mercy, I offer you this reflection in the hope that each of you may accompany me on the inner journey that I have been undertaking in recent weeks, so that we may be guided not by our interests or, even worse, by our wounded pride but rather by the Spirit with his gift.

At times, when similar evils damage our spirit and cast us into the world weak, fearful, shielded in our comfortable "winter palaces," God's love comes to meet us and to cleanse our intentions so that we may love as free, mature, and discerning men. When the communications media embarrass us by presenting a Church almost always under a new moon, bereft of the light of the Sun of justice (Saint Ambrose, *Hexameron* iv, 8:32) and we are tempted to doubt the paschal victory of the Risen One, I believe that, as Saint Thomas said, we must not be afraid of doubt (Jn 20:25) but must fear the insistent longing to see, not trusting the witness of those who have heard the most beautiful promise from the Lord's lips (Mt 28:20).

Today I ask you to speak not of certainties, but only of that which the Lord allows us to experience every day: joy, peace, forgiveness of our sins, and the action of his grace.

In this regard, I would like to express my gratitude to Archbishop Charles Scicluna of Malta and Msgr. Jorge Bertomeu Farnós, official of the Congregation for the Doctrine of Faith, for what they have accomplished in their calm and empathetic listening to the sixty-four depositions they collected recently both in New York and in Santiago de Chile. I sent them to listen from the heart and with humility. Afterwards, when they delivered their report to me, and especially in their juridical and pastoral assessment of the information gathered, they acknowledged that they had felt overwhelmed by the pain of so many victims of serious abuses of conscience and of power and, in particular, of sexual abuse committed against minors by various consecrated people in your country, which, denied at the time, robbed them of their innocence.

As pastors, we must express heartfelt and cordial gratitude to those who, with honesty, courage, and feeling for the Church, asked to meet my envoys and showed them the wounds in their very souls. Archbishop Scicluna and Msgr. Bertomeu told me that, with impressive maturity, respect, and amiability, several bishops, priests, deacons, laymen and laywomen of Santiago and Osorno met with them at Holy Name Parish in New York or Sotero Sanz, in Providencia.

Moreover, in the days following the Special Mission, they were witnesses to another fact worth keeping in mind for other occasions. Not only was the climate of confidentiality established during the visit maintained, but at no time did anyone succumb to the temptation to turn that sensitive mission into a media circus. In this respect, I would like to thank the various organizations and the media for their professionalism in dealing with this most delicate case, respecting the right of citizens to information and the good reputation of those testifying.

Now, after a careful reading of the report of the Special Mission, I believe I can state that all of the collected statements speak in a straightforward manner, without additives or sugarcoating, of many lives crucified, and I confess that this causes me sorrow and shame.

Taking all of this into account, I write to you, gathered at your 115th Plenary Assembly, in order to humbly request your cooperation and assistance in discerning the measures that must be adopted in the short, medium, and long term in order to restore ecclesial communion in Chile, remedy the scandal to the extent possible, and re-establish justice.

I intend to summon you to Rome in order to discuss the conclusions of the aforementioned report and my own conclusions. I have envisioned this encounter as a fraternal moment, colored by neither prejudice nor preconceived ideas, with the sole aim of making the truth shine forth in our lives. As to the date, I ask the Secretary of the Episcopal Conference to suggest a convenient time.

With regard to myself, I recognize, and I would like you to convey this faithfully, that I have made serious errors in the assessment and perception of the situation, in particular through the lack of reliable and balanced information. I now beg the forgiveness of all those whom I have offended and I hope to be able to do so personally, in the coming weeks, in the meetings that I will have with representatives of the people interviewed.

"Abide in me" (Jn 15:4): these words of the Lord continually resonate in these days. They speak of personal relationships, of communion, of fraternity that attracts and summons. United to Christ as branches to the vine, I invite you to instill in your prayers in the coming days a magnanimity that may prepare us for the above-mentioned meeting and allow us to transform into concrete acts all that we will have reflected upon. Now more than ever we cannot fall back into the temptation of verbosity and clinging to "universal" themes. In these days, let us look to Christ. Let us look to his life and his gestures, especially when he shows he is compassionate and merciful to those who have done wrong. Let us love truth. Let us ask for wisdom of heart and allow ourselves to undergo conversion.

I look forward to hearing from you and, asking Bishop Santiago Silva Retamales, President of the Episcopal Conference of Chile, to publish this letter as soon as possible, I impart to you my blessing and ask you, please, to never cease praying for me.

Francis

† LETTER TO THE BISHOPS OF CHILE
May 15, 2018

Dear Brothers,

On April 8, Mercy Sunday, I sent you a letter summoning you to Rome to discuss the conclusions of the visit carried out by the Special Mission, which had the task of helping to shed light on how to adequately treat an open, painful, and complex wound that has been bleeding for a long time in the lives of many people and, therefore, in the life of the people of God.

It is a wound treated thus far with medicine that, rather than healing it, seems to have made it even deeper and more painful. We must recognize that various actions have been taken with the aim of repairing the damage and suffering, but we must also be aware of the fact that the path followed has not been worth much for healing and curing. Maybe this was because of a wish to turn the page too quickly without taking responsibility for the unfathomable ramifications of this evil; or because the courage to face the responsibilities, omissions, and especially the permissive dynamics that allowed the wounds to occur and perpetuate themselves over time has disappeared; or perhaps because the resolve to take on the reality in which we are all involved—I first of all—and from which no one can exempt himself by moving the problem onto the shoulders of others, has been lacking; or because it was thought that it would be possible to move forward without recognizing, with humility and firmness, that mistakes had been made throughout the process.

After listening to the opinions of several people and perceiving the persistence of the wound, I established a special commission that, with great freedom of spirit, could reach as independent a diagnosis as possible in a juridical and technical way and cast a clear look on past events and the current state of the situation.

The time that is now offered to us is a time of grace. It is a time in which, under the inspiration of the Holy Spirit and in an atmosphere of collegiality, the necessary steps can be taken to generate the conversion to which the same Spirit wants to lead us. A change is needed; we know it, we need it, and we desire it. It is not only a debt that we have toward our communities and many people who have suffered and still suffer in their flesh the pains caused. The spirit of conversion is part of the very mission and identity of the Church. Let this be a time of conversion.

"He must increase, but I must decrease" (Jn 3:30). The last of the great prophets, John the Baptist, addressed these words to his disciples when, scandalized, they came to report that someone was doing the same things that he was doing. John, aware of his identity and his mission—he was not the Messiah, but he had been sent before him (v. 28)—did not hesitate to give them a clear answer, free from any ambiguity.

With this background of prophecy and inspired by the words of this prophet, I would like to initiate the fraternal reflection in which we will engage during these days.

He must increase...

Perhaps there is no greater joy for the believer than to share, witness, and make visible Jesus and his Kingdom. The encounter with the Risen One transforms life and makes faith become joyfully "contagious." It is the seed of the Kingdom of Heaven that tends spontaneously toward sharing, toward multiplying itself, and that leads us, like Andrew, to run toward our brothers and to say: "We have found the Messiah" (Jn 1:41): a Messiah who always opens up to us a horizon of life and hope. Through the action of the Spirit, the disciple allows himself to be launched on this adventure of making the new life that Jesus offers us grow and spread. We can never identify this action with proselytism or with the conquest of spaces; it is instead the joyful invitation to the new life that Jesus gives us. "He must increase" is what beats in the heart of the disciple, because he has experienced that Jesus Christ is the offer of good life. Only he is capable of saving.

The Church in Chile has experienced this. History tells us that it knew how to be a mother and gave birth to many in the faith, that it preached the new life of the Gospel and fought for it when it was threatened. This is a Church that has known how to "do battle" when the dignity of its children was not respected or was simply ignored. It did not seek to put itself at the center at all, it did not seek to be the center; it knew how to be the Church that put what was important at the center. In dark moments in the life of its people, the Church in Chile had the prophetic courage not only to raise its voice but also to create spaces for the defense of men and women whom the Lord had charged it to watch over. It knew well that the new commandment of love could not be proclaimed without promoting, through justice and peace, the true growth of every person.[1] Thus we can speak of a

---

1. Cf. Pope Paul VI, *Evangelii Nuntiandi*, n. 29.

prophetic Church that knows how to offer and generate the good life that the Lord has offered us.

A prophetic Church that knows how to put Jesus at the center is capable of promoting an evangelizing action that looks at the Master with the tenderness of Teresa of the Andes, and affirms: "Are you afraid of approaching him? Look at him in the midst of his faithful flock, while he carries the unfaithful sheep on his shoulders. Look at him at the tomb of Lazarus. And listen to him say to the Magdalene: much has been forgiven her because she loved very much. What do you discover in these passages of the Gospel if not a sweet, tender, compassionate heart, a heart, finally, of a God?"[2]

A prophetic Church that knows how to put Jesus at the center is capable of celebrating the joy induced by the Gospel. As I remarked in Iquique (but we can certainly apply this to many places in northern and southern Chile) popular piety is one of the greatest riches that the people of God have been able to cultivate. Traditional patronal festivals, with their religious dances—some of which last even for weeks—their music and their clothes transform many areas into sanctuaries of popular piety. In fact, these are not feasts that stay closed inside the church, but they manage to turn the whole town into a party.[3] And so an interconnectedness is created that is capable of celebrating the presence of God among his people in joy and hope. In the sanctuaries, we learn to be a Church of closeness, of listening, that knows how to feel and share life as it presents itself. A Church that has learned that faith

---

2. St. Teresa of the Andes, *Diarios y cartas*, 373; 376.

3. Pope Francis, "Homily for Mass of Our Lady of Mount Carmel and Prayer for Chile," Lobito Campus (Iquique), Chile (January 18, 2018).

is transmitted only in dialect and thus celebrates by singing and dancing "the fatherhood, the providence, the loving and constant presence of God."[4]

A prophetic Church that knows how to put Jesus at the center is capable of generating in holiness a man who was able to proclaim with his life: "Christ wanders our streets in the person of so many sick, suffering poor people, forced to abandon their wretched lodging. Christ, crouched under bridges, in the person of many children who have no one to call 'father,' who for many years have been deprived of a mother's kiss on their forehead... Christ does not have a home! Don't we want to give it to him?... 'What you do to the least of my brothers you do to me,' said Jesus."[5] In fact, "If we have truly started out anew from the contemplation of Christ, we must learn to see him especially in the faces of those with whom he himself wished to be identified."[6]

A prophetic Church that knows how to put Jesus at the center is capable of calling for the creation of spaces that accompany and defend the life of the different peoples that make up its vast territory, recognizing an unparalleled multicultural and ethnic wealth, which must be protected. As an example, I point out the initiatives promoted especially by the bishops of southern Chile in the 1960s, promoting the dynamics necessary for the Mapuche people to fully experience the art of living well, initiatives from which we have much to

---

4. Ibid.; cf. Pope Paul VI, *Evangelii Nuntiandi*, n. 48; CELAM, *Puebla*, nn. 400, 454; CELAM, *Aparecida*, nn. 99f, 262–265; Pope Francis, *Evangelii Gaudium*, n. 122.

5. St. Alberto Hurtado, *Cristo non ha dimora*, meditation during a retreat for women, October 16, 1944.

6. Pope St. John Paul II, *Novo Millennio Ineunte*, n. 49.

learn. Strong actions have generated structures favorable to the defense of life by calling people to become the responsible protagonists of an incarnate, transforming faith, a faith that knows how to give life to the call of the Council that reminds us that "the joys and the hopes, the griefs and the anxieties of the people of this age, especially those who are poor or in any way afflicted, these are the joys and hopes, the griefs and anxieties of the followers of Christ. Indeed, nothing genuinely human fails to raise an echo in their hearts."[7]

A prophetic Church that knows how to put Jesus at the center with sincerity is capable—as one of your pastors has been able to show us—of "confessing that, in our personal history and in the history of Chile, there have been injustice, lies, hatred, guilt, indifference." He invited you to be "sincere, humble, and to say to the Lord: we have sinned against you! To sin against our brother, man and woman, is to sin against Christ, who died and rose for all men. We are sincere, humble! Lord, I have sinned against you! I have not obeyed your Gospel!"[8] A conscience aware of its limitations and its sins makes us live alert to the temptation to supplant our Lord.

And so we could continue to enumerate many more vital aspects of the prophetic Church that knows how to put Jesus at the center. But the biggest and most fruitfully vital invitation —as I wanted to highlight when recalling St. Edith Stein in the recent Apostolic Exhortation—comes from the trust and conviction that "in the darkest night the greatest prophets and saints arise. But the life-giving current of mystical life remains

---

7. Vatican Council II, *Gaudium et Spes*, n. 1.

8. Silva Henríquez, *Reconciliación de los chilenos*, Homily at the conclusion of the Holy Year, November 24, 1974.

invisible. Certainly the decisive events of world history have been essentially influenced by souls about whom nothing is said in the history books. And which souls we must thank for the decisive events of our personal life is something that we will know only on the day when everything that is hidden will be revealed."[9] The faithful Holy People of God, in their daily silence, in many forms and many ways, continue to make visible and testify with "stubborn" hope that the Lord does not abandon, that he supports the constant self-giving and, in many situations, suffering of his children. The holy and patient faithful People of God, supported and given life by the Holy Spirit, make visible the best face of the prophetic Church that knows how to put its Lord at the center in daily self-giving.[10] Our attitude as shepherds consists in learning to trust in this ecclesial reality and to reverence and recognize the fact that in a simple people who confess their faith in Jesus Christ, love the Virgin, earn their living by work (often poorly paid), baptize their children, and bury their dead, in this faithful people who know themselves as sinners but never tire of seeking forgiveness because they believe in the Father's mercy, in this faithful and silent people resides the immune system of the Church.

...But I must decrease

It is painful to note that, in the most recent period of the history of the Chilean Church, this prophetic inspiration has lost

---

9. St. Edith Stein, *Verborgenes Leben und Epiphanie*, in GW XI, 145.

10. Cf. Pope Francis, *Gaudete et Exsultate*, nn. 6–9.

its vigor by giving way to what we could call a transformation at its center. I do not know what came first, if the loss of prophetic force led to the change of center or if the change of center led to the loss of prophecy that was so characteristic in you. But we can certainly observe that that Church which was called to point to the One who is the Way, the Truth, and the Life (Jn 14:6) has itself become the center of attention. It stopped looking and pointing to the Lord in order to look at itself and take care of itself. It concentrated its attention on itself and lost the memory of its origin and its mission.[11] It has focused on itself to such an extent that the consequences of this process have cost a very high price: *its sin has become the center of attention.* The painful and shameful occurrence of sexual abuse of minors, the abuse of power and of conscience by ministers of the Church, as well as the way in which these situations have been addressed,[12] give evidence of this "change of ecclesial center." Where, instead of the Church diminishing so that the signs of the Risen One may be seen, it was ecclesial sin that occupied the entire scene, directing attention and looks to itself.

It is urgent that we face this scandal and try to remedy it in the short, medium, and long term in order to restore justice

---

11. "Your fame spread among the nations on account of your beauty, for it was perfect because of my splendor that I had bestowed on you, says the Lord God. But you trusted in your beauty, and played the whore because of your fame" (Ez 16:14-15b).

12. In the report presented by the "special mission," it is symptomatic that all witnesses, including members of the National Council for the prevention of abuse of minors and for the accompaniment of victims, reported the insufficient pastoral attention paid until then to all those who had been involved, in one way or another, in a canonical cause relating to *delicta graviora.*

and communion.[13] At the same time, I believe that, with the same urgency, we must work at another level to discern how to generate new ecclesial dynamics in consonance with the Gospel, dynamics that will help us to be better missionary disciples capable of recovering prophecy.

The new life that the Lord gives us implies that the clarity of the Baptist must be recovered, and it insists without ambiguity that the disciple is not and will never be the Messiah. This leads us to promote a joyful and realistic awareness of ourselves: *the disciple is not greater than his Lord*. This means that, in the first place, we must be careful of any type or form of messianism that claims to stand as the sole interpreter of the will of God. Many times we can fall into the temptation of an ecclesial experience of authority that claims to supplant the various instances of communion and participation, or, even worse, to supplant the conscience of the faithful by forgetting the conciliar teaching that reminds us that "conscience is the most secret core and sanctuary of a man. There he is alone with God, whose voice echoes in his depths."[14] It is essential that we recover an ecclesial dynamic capable of helping disciples to discern God's dream for their lives, without pretending to supplant them in this search. In fact, false messianisms try to erase the eloquent truth that it is the entire body of the faithful that has the anointing of the Holy One.[15] Neither an individual nor an enlightened group can ever claim to be the totality of God's people, let alone believe themselves to be the authentic voice of its interpretation.

---

13. Cf. Pope Francis, "Letter to the Bishops of Chile" (April 8, 2018).

14. Vatican Council II, *Gaudium et Spes*, n. 16.

15. Cf. Vatican Council II, *Lumen Gentium*, n. 12.

Thus, we must guard against what I allow myself to call "elite psychology," which can appear in our way of dealing with questions.

Elite or elitist psychology ends up generating dynamics of division, separation, and "closed circles," which lead to a narcissistic and authoritarian spirituality where, instead of evangelizing, what matters is feeling special, different from others, thus indicating that neither Jesus Christ nor others are truly of any interest.[16] Messianisms, elitisms, and clericalisms are all symptoms of perversion in the ecclesial body. Also synonymous with perversion is the loss of the healthy awareness that we belong to the holy faithful People of God that precedes us and—thank God—will continue after us. May we never lose our awareness of that sublime gift that is our baptism.

It is the sincere, prayerful, and often even painful acknowledgment of our limits that allows grace to act more strongly in us, since it establishes the space that allows for that possible good that is inherent in a sincere, communal dynamic of real growth.[17] Awareness of the limitation and the partialness of our place within the people of God saves us from the temptation and the pretension of wanting to occupy all spaces, and especially a place that is not ours: that of the Lord. Only God is capable of the totality, only he is capable of the totality of an exclusive and at the same time not-excluding love. Our mission is and will always be a shared mission. As I told you at the meeting with the clergy of Santiago, "The knowledge that we are wounded sets us free. Yes, it sets us free from becoming self-referential and thinking ourselves superior. It sets us free from the promethean tendency

---

16. Cf. Pope Francis, *Evangelii Gaudium*, n. 94.
17. Cf. Pope Francis, *Gaudete in Exsultate*, n. 52.

LETTER TO THE BISHOPS OF CHILE (MAY 15, 2018)

of those who ultimately trust only in their own powers and feel superior to others."[18]

Therefore, and allow me to insist, it is urgent that we generate ecclesial dynamics capable of promoting the participation and shared mission of all the members of the ecclesial community, avoiding any type of messianism or elite psychology-spirituality. And, in concrete terms, for example, it will do us good to open ourselves more and work together with different components of civil society to promote a three-hundred-sixty-degree anti-abuse culture.

When I summoned you to this meeting, I invited you to ask the Spirit for the gift of magnanimity in order to be able to translate into concrete actions the points on which we would reflect. I urge you to implore this gift insistently for the good of the Church in Chile. I have perceived with some concern the attitude with which some of you, bishops, have reacted to present and past events. It is an attitude oriented toward what we could call the "Jonah episode"—in the midst of the storm it was deemed necessary to throw the problem overboard (Jonah 1:4-16)[19]—in the belief that the mere removal of people would in itself solve the problems.[20] Here we see a forgetting of the Pauline principle: "If the foot would say, 'Because I am not a hand, I do not belong to the body,'

---

18. Pope Francis, Meeting with priests, consecrated men and women, and seminarians, Santiago Cathedral (January 16, 2018).

19. Jonah himself admits that the storm was caused by the fact that he had not taken up the mission that he was called to, and that to escape it they had to throw him overboard: "Pick me up and throw me into the sea; then the sea will quiet down for you; for I know it is because of me that this great storm has come upon you" (v. 12).

20. "When the dog died, the rabies went away." We could also speak of the "Caiaphas syndrome": "It is fitting that one man die for the people."

that would not make it any less a part of the body" (1 Cor 12:15). The problems that are experienced today within the ecclesial community are not solved only by tackling concrete cases and reducing them to the removal of people.[21] This—and I say it clearly—must be done, but it is not enough; we must go further. It would be irresponsible of us *not to go deeper* in seeking the roots and structures that have allowed these concrete events to happen and perpetuate themselves. The painful situations that have occurred are indicative of the fact that something is wrong with the ecclesial body.[22] We must deal with concrete cases and, at the same time—and with the same intensity—go deeper to discover the dynamics that made possible the occurrence of similar attitudes and evils.[23] Confessing sin is necessary; trying to remedy it is urgent; understanding its roots is wisdom for the present and the future. It would be a serious omission on our part not to go to the roots. Furthermore, believing that only removing

---

21. Because we are not dealing with just one particular case. There are numerous situations of abuse of power, of authority, of sexual abuse. And these include the way they have been handled so far.

22. For example, in the report presented by the Special Mission, many of those interviewed in the Nunciature claim that part of the deep fracture in ecclesial communion among the clergy would be brought with them from the seminary, spoiling what should be priestly fraternal relations and making the faithful participants in these divisions and fractures, which end up irreparably damaging the social credibility and ecclesial authority of priests and bishops.

23. In the report of the Special Mission, my envoys were able to confirm that after some religious were expelled from their orders because of the immorality of their conduct and the absolute seriousness of their criminal acts had been minimized by attributing them to simple weakness or moral lack, they were welcomed in other dioceses and, even more imprudently, were entrusted with diocesan or parish assignments that involved daily and direct contact with minors.

people, and nothing more, would restore the health of the body is a big mistake. There is no doubt that it would help and that it is necessary to do it, but I repeat that it is not enough,[24] because this approach would dispense us from the responsibility and the participation that is expected of us within the ecclesial body. And where responsibility is not accepted and shared, the blame for what does not work is al-

---

24. With regard to this, I would like to focus on three situations discussed in the report of the Special Mission:

The investigation shows that there are serious flaws in the handling of cases of *delicta graviora*, which corroborates troubling data that had begun to be known in some Roman dicasteries—especially in the way of receiving complaints, or "*notitiae criminis*," since in many cases serious indications of an actual crime were superficially classified as improbable. During the visit, the existence of alleged crimes that were investigated inattentively or were never investigated at all was also ascertained, with the consequent scandal for those who had reported them and for all those who knew the alleged victims: families, friends, parish communities. In other cases, the existence of very serious negligence in the protection of vulnerable boys and girls by religious bishops and superiors, who have a special responsibility in the task of protecting the people of God, has been noted.

Another similar circumstance that caused me perplexity and shame was reading the declarations that certify pressure was exerted on those who had to conduct criminal trials, or even the destruction of compromising documents by those in charge of ecclesiastical archives, thus demonstrating an absolute lack of respect for canonical procedure and, still more, reprehensible practices that must be avoided in the future.

Along the same lines, and confirming the fact that the problem does not concern only one group of people, many abusers were identified as serious problems dating back to the stage of formation in the seminary or novitiate. In fact, in the documents of the Special Mission, there are serious accusations against some bishops or superiors who allegedly entrusted educational institutions to priests suspected of active homosexuality.

ways placed on someone else.[25] Please, let us avoid the temptation to want to save ourselves, save our reputation ("save our own skin"); rather, let us confess our weakness communally, in order to find, together, answers that are humble, concrete, and in communion with all the people of God. The gravity of the incident does not allow us to pose as expert "scapegoat hunters." All this requires of us seriousness and co-responsibility to take on the problems as symptoms of an ecclesial whole that we are invited to analyze. It also requires us to seek all the necessary mediations so that such things never happen again. We can do this only if we understand this as everyone's problem and not just the problem of some. We can solve the problem only if we take it on collegially, in communion, in synodality.

Brothers, we are not here because we are better than others. As I said to you in Chile, we are here with the awareness of being forgiven sinners or sinners who want to be forgiven, sinners in a position of penitential openness. And in this we will find the source of our joy. We want to be shepherds after the wounded, dead, and risen Jesus. We want to find in the wounds of our people the signs of the Resurrection. We want to move from being a Church centered on itself, broken down and desolate because of its sins, to being a Church that serves the many disheartened people who live alongside us. *A Church capable of placing at the center what is important*: the

---

25. This paradigmatic attitude reminds us of Genesis 3:11–13: "'Have you eaten from the tree of which I commanded you not to eat?' The man said, 'The woman whom you gave to be with me, she gave me fruit from the tree, and I ate.' Then the Lord God said to the woman, 'What is this that you have done?' The woman said, 'The serpent tricked me, and I ate.'" It reminds us of the attitude of the child who looks at its parents and says, "It wasn't me."

service of its Lord in the hungry, the prisoner, the thirsty, the homeless, the naked, the sick, the abused ... (Mt 25:35), with an awareness that they have the dignity of sitting at our tables, of feeling "at home" among us, of being considered family. This is the sign that the Kingdom of Heaven is among us. It is the sign of a Church that has been wounded by its sin, experienced mercy from its Lord, and made prophetic by vocation.[26] Brothers, ideas are discussed, situations are discerned. We are gathered to discern, not to discuss.

To restore prophecy is to refocus ourselves on what is important; it is to look upon the one they have pierced and to be told, "He is not here; for he has been raised" (Mt 28:6); it is to create the conditions and ecclesial dynamics so that each person, in the situation in which they find themselves, can discover the one who Lives and awaits us in Galilee.

Francis

---

26. Cf. Pope Francis, Meeting with priests, consecrated men and women, and seminarians, Santiago Cathedral (January 16, 2018).

Letter to the Bishops of Chile
May 17, 2018

Dear Brothers in the Episcopate,

I wish to thank you for having accepted this invitation so that, together, we have been able to carry out a frank discernment regarding the grave events that have damaged ecclesial communion and weakened the work of the Church of Chile in recent years.

In light of these painful events regarding abuses—of minors, of power, and of conscience—we have examined their seriousness and their tragic consequences, particularly for the victims. To some of them I myself made a heartfelt plea for forgiveness, to which you have joined in a single will and with the firm intention of repairing the damage caused.

I thank you for the full willingness each one of you has shown to adhere to and collaborate in all the changes and resolutions we will have to implement in the short, medium, and long term in order to restore justice and ecclesial communion.

After these days of prayer and reflection, I ask you to continue building a prophetic Church, one that knows how to restore to the center what is important: service to your Lord in the hungry, in the prisoner, in the migrant, and in the abused.

Please, do not forget to pray for me.

May Jesus bless you and the Holy Virgin take care of you.

Fraternally,

Francis

† LETTER TO THE PILGRIM PEOPLE OF GOD IN CHILE
May 31, 2018

Dear Brothers and Sisters,

This past April 8, I called my brother bishops to Rome to seek together in the short, medium, and long term the ways of truth and life in the face of an open, painful, and complex wound that for a long time has not stopped bleeding.¹ And I suggested that the bishops invite the entire faithful Holy People of God to engage in prayer that the Holy Spirit might give us the strength to not fall into the temptation of getting caught up in empty word games, in sophisticated diagnoses, or in vain gestures that would prevent us from having the courage to look directly at the pain that has been caused, the face of its victims, and the magnitude of what has taken place. I invited them to look to where the Holy Spirit is moving us, since "closing our eyes to our neighbor also blinds us to God."²

With joy and hope I received the news that there were many communities, towns, and chapels where the People of God were praying, especially on the days when we were gathered together with the bishops: the People of God on their knees, imploring the gift of the Holy Spirit to find the light in the Church, "wounded by her sin, granted mercy by her Lord,

---

1. Cf. Letter of the Holy Father Francis to the Bishops of Chile following the report of His Excellency Archbishop Charles J. Scicluna (April 8, 2018).

2. Benedict XVI, *Deus Caritas Est*, n. 16.

so that every day she may become prophetic in her vocation."³ We know that prayer is never in vain and that "in the midst of darkness something new always buds forth, that sooner or later bears fruit."⁴

1. To appeal to you, to ask for your prayers was not a practical recourse nor was it a simple goodwill gesture. On the contrary, I wanted to frame things in their precise and meaningful place and put the issue where it ought to be: the essential condition of the People of God is "the dignity and freedom of the sons of God, in whose hearts the Holy Spirit dwells as in His temple."⁵ The faithful Holy People of God are anointed with the grace of the Holy Spirit; therefore, when we reflect, think, evaluate, and discern we must be very attentive to this anointing. Whenever as a Church, as pastors, as consecrated persons, we have forgotten this, we have lost our way. Whenever we try to supplant, silence, look down on, ignore, or reduce into small elites the People of God in their totality and differences, we construct communities, pastoral plans, theological approaches, spiritualities, structures without roots, without history, without faces, without memory, without a body—in the end, without lives. To remove ourselves from the life of the People of God hastens us to desolation and to a perversion of ecclesial nature; the fight against a culture of abuse requires us to renew our awareness of the nature of the People of God.

As I said to the young people in Maipú, I want especially to tell each one of you: "Holy Mother the Church today

---

3. Cf. Meeting of the Holy Father Francis with priests, men and women religious, consecrated men and women, seminarians, Cathedral of Santiago de Chile, January 16, 2018.

4. Cf. Francis, *Evangelii Gaudium,* n. 278.

5. Cf. Vatican Council II, *Lumen Gentium,* n. 9.

needs the faithful People of God to challenge us...The Church needs you to take out your adult ID card, as spiritual adults, and have the courage to tell us 'I like this,' 'This is the way I think we should go,' 'That's not going to work,'...Tell us what you feel and think."[6] In this manner all of us can be involved in a Church with a synodal character that knows how to put Jesus in the center.

The People of God does not have first, second, or third-class Christians. Their participation is not a matter of goodwill or concessions; rather, it is constitutive of the nature of the Church. It is not possible to imagine a future without this anointing operating in each one of the faithful, which certainly demands and requires new forms of participation. I urge all Christians not to be afraid to be the protagonists of the transformation that is demanded today, and to promote and enliven creative alternatives in the daily search for a Church that wants always to put what is important in the center. I invite all diocesan organizations from whatever area they may be to search consciously and credibly for areas of communion and participation so that the anointing of the People of God may find concrete ways of expressing itself.

The renewal of the Church hierarchy by itself does not create the transformation to which the Holy Spirit moves us. We are required to promote together a transformation of the Church that involves us all.

A Church that is prophetic, and therefore, full of hope, demands of everyone an eyes-wide-open mysticism that questions, that is not asleep.[7] Do not let yourselves be robbed of the anointing of the Spirit.

---

6. Cf. Meeting of the Holy Father Francis with young people at National Shrine of Maipú, January 28, 2017.

7. Cf. Francis, *Gaudate et Exsultate*, n. 96.

2. "The wind blows where it will, and you can hear the sound it makes, but you do not know where it comes from or where it goes; so it is with everyone who is born of the Spirit" (Jn 3:8). This is how Jesus responded to Nicodemus in the conversation they had on the possibility of being born again in order to enter the Kingdom of Heaven.

At this time and in the light of this passage it is good for us to look back at our personal and communal history. The Holy Spirit blows where and how he wills with the sole purpose of helping us to be born again. Far from letting us get boxed up in schemes, modalities, fixed or obsolete structures, far from letting ourselves be resigned or "letting down our guard" in the face of events, the Spirit is continually in movement to widen our horizons, to make the person who has lost hope[8] able to dream, to do justice in truth and charity, to be purified of sin and corruption, and always ready to welcome necessary conversion. Without this faith perspective, everything we could say or do would be useless. Such a perspective is essential if we are to look at the present without evasion but with bravery, with courage but with wisdom, with tenacity but without violence, with passion but without fanaticism, with constancy but without anxiety and thus change all that which today puts at risk the integrity and dignity of every person. The solutions that are needed demand facing the problems without getting trapped in them or—what would be worse—repeating the same courses of action that we want to eliminate.[9] Today we are challenged to look straight ahead,

---

8. Cf. Francis, Homily at Solemnity of Pentecost Mass, 2018.

9. It is good to recognize some of the organizations and media that have taken up the issue of abuse in a responsible way, always seeking the truth and not making out of this painful reality a means to boost program ratings.

face and suffer the conflict, and thus be able to resolve and transform it so as to move in a new direction.[10]

3. First of all, it would be unfair to ascribe this process simply to recently experienced events. Every process of review and purification that we are experiencing has been made possible thanks to the efforts and perseverance of specific individuals, who even against all hope or while enduring the pain of not being believed, did not tire of seeking the truth; I am referring to the victims of sexual abuse, of abuse of power and authority, and to those who at the time believed and accompanied them, victims whose cry reached the heavens.[11] I would like once more publicly to thank all of them for their courage and perseverance.

This recent period has been a time of listening and discernment to discover the root of the problem, what it was that allowed such atrocities to occur and be perpetuated, and thus to find solutions to the abuse scandal, not merely by means of containment strategies—essential but insufficient—but with the measures necessary to take on the entire problem in all its complexity.

In this regard I would like to pause on the word "listening," since discerning requires learning how to listen to what the Spirit wants to tell us. And we will be able to do that only if we are capable of listening to the reality of what is going on.[12]

---

10. Cf. Francis, *Evangelii Gaudium*, n. 227.

11. "The Lord said 'I have witnessed the affliction of my people in Egypt and have heard their cry against their taskmasters, so I know well what they are suffering'" (Ex 3:7).

12. Let us remember that this was the first word-commandment that the people of Israel received from Yahweh: "Listen, Israel" (Dt 6:4).

I believe that here lies one of our main faults and omissions: not knowing how to listen to the victims. As a result, conclusions drawn were only partial and lacked the crucial elements needed for healthy and clear discernment. With shame, I must say that we did not know how to listen and react in time.

The visit of Archbishop Scicluna and Monsignor Bertomeu resulted from the realization that there were situations that we did not know how to see and hear. As a Church, we could not continue to walk in ignorance of the pain of our brothers. After reading the report, I wanted to meet personally with some of the victims of sexual abuse, the abuse of power, and the abuse of conscience, to listen to them and to ask forgiveness for our sins and omissions.

4. In these meetings, I came to see how the lack of recognition/ listening to their stories, as well as the lack of recognition/ acceptance of the errors and omissions in the entire process impedes us from making headway. A necessary recognition ought to be more than an expression of goodwill toward the victims; rather, it should to be a way for us to adopt a new attitude before life, before others, and before God. Hope for tomorrow and confidence arise from and grow in taking on fragility, limitations, and even sin in order to help us move forward.[13]

The "never again" to the culture of abuse and the system of cover-up that allows it to be perpetuated demands working with everyone in order to generate a culture of care that permeates our ways of relating, praying, and thinking; our ways of living authority, our customs and languages, and our relationship with power and money. We know today that the best

---

13. Cf. Visit of the Holy Father Francis to the Women's Correctional Center, Santiago de Chile, January 16, 2018.

thing we can do in face of the pain that has been caused is to commit ourselves to personal, communal, and social conversion that learns to listen to and care, especially for the most vulnerable. It is therefore urgent that we create spaces where a culture of abuse and cover-up is not the norm, where a critical and questioning attitude is not confused with betrayal. We have to promote this as a Church and to seek out with humility all who take part in the social reality, to promote ways of dialogue and constructive confrontation that can help us move toward a culture of care and protection.

To attempt this enterprise by ourselves alone, or only with our own efforts and tools, would shut us up in a dangerous voluntaristic dynamic that would perish in the short term.[14] Let us allow ourselves to be helped and to help create a society in which the culture of abuse does not find the space to perpetuate itself. I exhort all Christians and especially those responsible for centers of higher education, whether formal or informal, healthcare centers, or institutes of formation and universities, to join together with the dioceses and with all of civil society to lucidly and strategically promote a culture of care and protection. Let each of these spaces promote a new mentality.

5. The culture of abuse and cover-up is incompatible with the logic of the Gospel, since the salvation offered by Christ is always an offer, a gift that demands and requires freedom. Washing the feet of the disciples is how Christ shows us the face of God. It is never by way of coercion or obligation but only by way of service. Let us say it clearly: every means that attacks freedom and a person's integrity is anti-Gospel.

---

14. Cf. Francis, *Gaudete et Exsultate*, nn. 47–59.

Therefore we must create processes of faith through which we can learn when it is necessary to doubt and when it is not. "Doctrine, or better our understanding and expression of it, 'is not a closed system, deprived of dynamics capable of bringing up questions, doubts, questionings,' since the questions of our people, their anxieties, their fights, their dreams, their struggles, possess a hermeneutical value that we cannot ignore if we want to take seriously the principle of incarnation."[15] I invite all centers of religious formation, theology schools, institutes of higher learning, seminaries, houses of formation and spirituality to promote a form of theological reflection that is capable of rising to the challenge of the present time to promote a mature, adult faith that assumes the vital and fertile soil of the People of God with their searching and questioning. And thus, to then promote communities capable of fighting against abusive situations, communities in which exchanges, debate, and confrontation are welcome.[16]

---

15. Cf. Francis, *Gaudete et Exsultate*, 44.

16. It is essential to carry out the much needed renovation in the centers of formation promoted by the recent Apostolic Constitution Veritates Gaudium. By way of example, I emphasize that "in fact, the urgent task of our time is that the entire People of God prepare themselves to embark on a new stage of 'Spirit-filled' evangelization. This calls for 'a resolute process of discernment, purification, and reform.' In this process a fitting renewal of the system of ecclesiastical studies plays a strategic role. These studies, in fact, are called to offer opportunities and processes for the suitable formation of priests, consecrated men and women, and committed lay people. At the same time, they are called to be a sort of providential cultural laboratory in which the Church carries out the performative interpretation of the reality brought about by the Christ event and nourished by the gifts of wisdom and knowledge by which the Holy Spirit enriches the People of God in manifold ways—from the sensus fidei fidelium to the magisterium of the

LETTER TO THE PILGRIM PEOPLE OF GOD IN CHILE (MAY 31, 2018)

We will be fruitful to the extent that we empower and open communities from within and thus free ourselves from closed and self-referential thoughts full of promises and mirages that promise life but that ultimately favor the culture of abuse.

I would like to make a brief reference to the pastoral ministry of popular devotion carried out in many of your communities, since it is an invaluable treasure and authentic school where we can learn to listen to the heart of our people and, at the same time, the heart of God. In my experience as a pastor I learned that pastoral ministry of popular devotion is one of the few places where the People of God is free from the influence of that clericalism that seeks always to control and block God's anointing of his people. Learning from popular devotion is a way of learning how to enter into a new kind of relationship of listening and spirituality that requires respect and does not lend itself to quick and simplistic readings, since popular piety "reflects a thirst for God that only the poor and simple can know."[17]

To be "the Church that goes out" is also to be a Church that is helped and challenged. Let us not forget that "the wind blows where it will: you hear its sound but you do not know where it comes from or where it is going. So it is with everyone born of the Spirit." (Jn 3:8)

6. As I mentioned, during my meetings with the victims I was able to see that the failure to recognize them as victims prevents us from getting anywhere. That is why I think it is necessary to

---

bishops, and from the charism of the prophets to that of the doctors and theologians." Francis, *Veritates Gaudium*, n. 3.

17. Paul VI, *Evangelii Nuntiandi*, n. 48.

share with you that it brought me joy and hope to confirm in conversation with them their recognition of those people I like to call "the saints next door."[18] It would be unfair if, alongside our pain and our shame for those structures of abuse and cover-up that have been so perpetuated and have done so much evil, we were to fail to recognize the many faithful lay people, consecrated men and women, priests and bishops who give life through love in the most remote areas of the beloved land of Chile. All of them are Christians who know how to weep with those who weep, who hunger and thirst for justice, who look and act with mercy;[19] Christians who try every day to illumine their lives in light of the standards by which we will be judged: "Come, you who are blessed by my Father. Inherit the kingdom prepared for you from the foundation of the world. For I was hungry and you gave me food, I was thirsty and you gave me drink, a stranger and you welcomed me, naked and you clothed me, ill and you cared for me, in prison and you visited me" (Mt 25:34–36).

I recognize and am thankful for their courage and constant example. In turbulent, shameful, and painful moments they have continued to stand with joy for the Gospel. Their witness does me great good and sustains me in my own desire to overcome selfishness, to give more fully of myself.[20] Far from diminishing the importance and seriousness of the evil and the need to seek out the causes of the problem, it also commits us to recognize the action and power of the Holy Spirit in so many lives. By ignoring this we would be taking only halfway measures, operating from a position that, far

---

18. Cf. Francis, *Gaudete et Exsultate*, nn. 6–9.

19. Ibid., nn. 76, 79, 82.

20. Cf. Francis *Evangelii Gaudium*, n. 76.

from empowering what is good and remedying what is wrong, would minimize the reality, leading to grave injustice.

Accepting the successes, as well as the personal and communal limitations, far from being just one more news item, becomes the initial step of every authentic process of conversion and transformation. Let us never forget that the risen Jesus Christ reveals himself with his wounds to those who are his own. Moreover, it is precisely because of his wounds that Thomas can confess his faith. We are called to not dissimulate, hide, or cover over our wounds.

A wounded Church is able to understand and be moved by the wounds of today's world, make them its own, suffer them, accompany them, and move to heal them. A wounded Church does not put itself at the center, does not think it is perfect, does not seek to cover up and dissimulate its evil, but places there the only one who can heal the wounds, and he has a name: Jesus Christ.[21]

It is this that will move us to seek, in season and out of season, the commitment to create a culture where each person has the right to breathe an air free of every kind of abuse; a culture free of the cover-ups that end up vitiating all our relationships; a culture that in being faced with sin creates a dynamic of repentance, mercy, and forgiveness, and faced with crime, denounces it, judges it, and imposes sanctions on it.

7. Dear brothers, I began this letter by telling you that my appeal to you is not simply a practical recourse or a gesture of goodwill; on the contrary, it is meant to invoke the anointing which as the People of God you possess. With you the

---

21. Cf. Meeting of the Holy Father Francis with priests, men and women religious, consecrated men and women, seminarians, Cathedral of Santiago de Chile, January 16, 2018.

necessary steps for ecclesial renewal and conversion can be taken, steps that will be decisive and lasting. With you the necessary transformation of that which is needed can be generated. Without you nothing can be done. I exhort all the faithful Holy People of God who live in Chile to be unafraid to get involved and to go forward moved by the Holy Spirit in search of a Church that is increasingly synodal, prophetic, and hopeful; less abusive because it knows how to place Jesus at the center, among the hungry, the prisoner, the migrant, and the abused.

I ask you not to cease praying for me. I pray for you and I ask Jesus to bless you and the Virgin to care for you.

Francis

Vatican May 31, 2018, Feast of the Visitation of Our Lady

POPE FRANCIS

"Eradicating the Culture of Abuse"

LETTER TO THE PEOPLE OF GOD

Guide to Reading the Letter to the People of God

James Hanvey, SJ

Pope Francis's "Letter to the People of God" marks a definitive moment in the Church's life. When placed alongside his letter of April 8 to the Chilean bishops' conference, it is an example of inspired leadership that has all the marks of his papacy: it is pastoral, practical, spiritual, and prophetic. The pope decries "the deep wounds of pain," in the victims and in the Church, arising from sexual abuse perpetrated by priests, bishops, and cardinals, and asks for a profound transformation of hierarchical and presbyteral culture. This is a task that can be accomplished only by the whole People of God.

In recent months, the inexorable weight of suffering caused by abuse in the Church in all its forms has broken into the light. So too has the reality that the Church, for whatever motives, colluded with abusers to try to silence victims and hide the truth. How could any group in the Church ever think that protecting itself was of greater service to God than recognizing the vast well of pain and destroyed lives—lives of the innocent faithful? How could a Church defend the dignity of the human person and claim to be the advocate for the poor and powerless, the voice of the voiceless, and the memory for the forgotten ones when it was itself as adroit as any secular State in suppressing the cry of those it claimed to love and cherish? If the justification was to prevent scandal from undermining the faith of the People of God, who was being protected, the Church or the clerical caste? It is in this context, and with these questions legitimately being asked, that Pope Francis has written his letter to the People of God.

Some will think it just more pious words, understandably doubting if the call to penance and prayer is adequate given the enormity of the crisis and the depth of pain that it has caused and continues to cause. Yet Francis has shown by his actions that he is not in the business of rhetoric. The letter hears the cry of the victims, too long muffled, silenced, or denied, and speaks to the truth of clerical abuse in the Church, which must have been present even beyond the seventy years mapped by the Pennsylvania grand jury report. It would be a mistake to think that such abuse could be localized to America, Chile, the UK, or Europe. The pope's letter is not a political strategy, an admission of guilt in the hope that the issue can be defused, contained, and forgotten once public attention is distracted by the next shock or event. Francis is not a politician; he is a servant of God and God's Church. The Church, like those who have suffered abuse, cannot "just move on." The reality of abuse and its truth—always a deeply personal one—must erupt into the present and rupture it; it cannot be tamed or wrapped in words and consigned to history. To do so would be the greatest betrayal of all. The Spirit does not play politics or deal in deception and distraction. The coin of the Spirit is truth: the truth about God and the truth about us. Pope Francis has discerned that in the visibility and voice of those who are suffering, the Spirit is speaking. If we do not listen and then respond beyond the necessary protocols and legal instruments, the Church will miss the grace that is being offered. It will run the risk of making itself and its own survival an end in itself, succumbing to the temptation of institutional idolatry.

In trying to be attentive to the Spirit's voice and presence, I believe Francis's letter marks a definitive moment from which there can be no turning back. The letter not only recognizes the victims of clerical abuse and the culture that perpetuates it, it describes the desolation in which the Church lives because of it. Yet, the pope's letter is not a letter of desolation; it is one of consolation. The Spirit breathes through its pages.

The Spirit of Witness

In the voices of all those who have been abused, the Spirit bears witness against the abusers and speaks for their victims. This is why the first response of the Church is not to rob them of their voice and their testimony. The first work of a Church genuine in its desire for conversion and repentance is to listen. This is often the hardest work of all. To analyze, categorize, and bureaucratize the testimony of anyone who has been or is being abused is another act of violence. Their unique history is translated and retold in other narratives that they no longer control. Their voice is lost, their face made anonymous. If the

Church really cares and sincerely desires to change, then it must listen to and honor each abused person. It must give space and time, for only then can it begin to hear, within the history of each person's suffering, what has been taken from them and all those down the years who have been hidden.

Abuse is not just one moment or even multiple moments of violence, manipulation, deception, and subjection. It enters the soul as well as the heart and mind. It is a rupture in the self and the fundamental sense of security on which identity depends. Abuse, even when buried, still has the power to hijack, destroy, and undermine a life. It cannot be easily or conveniently "healed" because the life of the person—their identity and confidence in themselves and their relationships—is always under threat. Often, in the case of clerical abuse, either the way in which the abuser has imposed their power or used the very formulas of faith to conceal and bind the person they are abusing, make the language of spirituality or the sacraments themselves sites of destructive memory and recall. This is why we must be very cautious about rushing to invoke such discourses as sources of understanding or promote them as strategies for recovery. The predatory abuser has already populated them, and they can be contaminated for the person who has been abused. Indeed, they may also be a symptom of the very clerical culture that has willingly or unwillingly allowed abuse to remain possible.

The testimony of those who have been abused will now always be part of the Church's identity. Their perseverance and courage is a *kairos* of conversion and renewal for the Church. The witness carried by the suffering of those who have been abused and their unmasking of its cause is certainly a source of desolation, but it is not disabling. It grounds the Church against the idolatry that places the institutional reputation before the lives of God's people. Without this witness, the Church loses the truth that is the very freedom and joy of its life, the condition of its mission. The Church cannot guarantee its own existence or survival: it lives always from Christ and the life-giving Spirit. Only when it rejoices in its own poverty is it free to serve Christ and him alone.

The deepest threat to such freedom is fear: fear of acknowledging sin and corruption; fear of losing influence and security; fear of losing control and power. In all his writings, Francis highlights this temptation. This is why the Church needs to live constantly beyond itself in sacrifice and self-giving love for the life of the world. As Vatican II saw clearly in *Lumen Gentium*, this is not only the form of discipleship that shapes every Christian life, it is the form of the holiness to which we are all called, whatever direction our lives and relationships may take. It is especially the case for vocations to priesthood and religious life.

Clericalism pretends to protect the sacrament of priesthood; in fact, it instrumentalizes it, placing it not at the disposal of God or the community but purely for the benefit of self. This is the great temptation of every gift of office, secular or ecclesial, and the only way of resisting it is to seek to live with an interior knowledge of one's own poverty, the habitus of humility and gratitude for the gift with which one has been entrusted. This is what is visible in the lives of so many priests and religious (women and men) spent in the "widow's mite" of mundane service. In this sense, conversion is not a sudden moment but a life-long process that requires prayer (in good times, bad times and boring times), honesty, humility, courage, and faith. The deeper the love we have for Christ and the world created and redeemed in him, the more we will wish to remove whatever is an obstacle to him and his work. Under the dynamic power of this love, the Church will constantly ask the Spirit to renew and dilate its life that it may live more fully the *semper maior* of a cruciform love. This is the process that Francis has been speaking about in all of his writings and homilies. He understands that the Church is not just an institutional structure but one that is made up of people. If the structures are relationships and these relationships are to reflect the economy of God's truth, mercy, and love, then that economy must be rooted in the lives and relationships of all its members.

The Spirit of Remembering and Intercession

The Spirit is the one who calls all things to mind and in that act also intercedes. In "remembering" the Holy Spirit takes our narrative and places it within that of Christ's narrative, salvation history. As the psalmist says, "In your light we see light." The transpositional and interpretive work of the Spirit makes the reconciling and liberating grace of Christ accessible and active within the tortured history of humanity. In such a way the Spirit guarantees the ultimate justice of God, for no innocent suffering is ever lost or devalued; it is illuminated and shines in the darkness. In the crucified and risen Christ, the Church sees every victim and their wounds, and through the action of the Holy Spirit, every celebration of Eucharist is an *anamnesis* of him and them made present before us and in every moment that has gone before or still to come. It is, indeed, a dangerous memory, for it subverts the strategies of avoidance and suppression. It reverses the values of all the hierarchies of power and, as the letter of Pope Francis makes clear, the Lord shows us "on which side he stands." Whenever the priest who abuses celebrates the Eucharist he stands in this penetrating light which exposes all that is hidden; he encounters this Lord and in him the victims of his own abuse.

Through the epiclesis of the Spirit, the whole community is present both in witness and in intercession, for the Spirit is also the creator of this solidarity. Solidarity means that we take on not the guilt of the perpetrator but the suffering of the victims, resolving to hear their cry and seek justice for them; we become their advocates in prayer and in life. In this way, we can begin to experience the deep grace of the Church's life and its hope: the real *communio* of the saints for whom intercession is a real work of repair. The faith-full community of Eucharist and intercession brings to the long, obscure, and crooked road of history a healing and guiding light, already a sign that the Kingdom is present. We cannot love Christ unless we love his Church, no matter how disfigured and weak, yet never abandoned by the Spirit that dwells with the community and, like the *Shekinah*, fills it with a glory that will heal the world.

The Spirit of Consolation and New Life

There are no barriers for the Holy Spirit. Even the secular world that maintains that it has no place for God cannot be immune to the Spirit. It can even be the Spirit's instrument. Is it not this secular world that has held the Church accountable when it could not do so for itself? Is it not the secular courts and agencies that have taught the Church the necessity of transparency, without which there can be no credibility? Through these institutes of the State, the Spirit is teaching the Church "to say an emphatic 'no' to all forms of clericalism." The secular world, too, calls the Church to conversion: to be a Church it can trust and believe.

At the risk of some distorting generalization, up to now the Church has relied on technical changes to deal with the abuse crisis: procedures, protocols, legal structures, and so forth. These are necessary, but they will not change a culture; they are the necessary signs of conversion, but they are not conversion itself. Indeed, they may become substitutes for it. The pope is engaged in something much more difficult: he is asking for the profound adaptive change that conversion requires. Such adaptive change is no threat to the essence and the truth of the Church; it recovers it.

Francis is asking us to go much further than safeguarding programs, procedures, and disciplinary structures, essential though they undoubtedly are. The pope, servant of the Council, recognizes that we must renew ecclesial culture, creating a priesthood and episcopacy that are conformed to the sacrament upon which they are based. New structures will need to be developed that give this expression, embody justice and compassion, and protect all parties from falsehood and exploitation. These structures will need to reflect an effective subsidiarity within the life of the Church and an openness to expertise irrespective of gender or ecclesial status. The Spirit must be allowed to penetrate every aspect of the Church's life, and this will require a willingness to discern and learn from all sources. This is the adaptive change of conversion that embeds a new habitus. Such change is always the most difficult and painful. Often it will put those who advocate it or lead it at risk of rejection or scapegoating. It requires us to face the truth and not shift the blame; it obliges us not to short-circuit the process with "quick fixes" to avoid pain or embarrassment. It moves us to another level of perception and understanding, to step out beyond what is familiar and comfortable, to let our minds and hearts be renewed until we begin to have "the mind of Christ." This takes time; it requires the grace of fortitude and perseverance, but also faith in God's people and the charisms that the Spirit has so richly bestowed upon them.

There will be many who wish to resist the adaptive change of conversion to which Pope Francis and those who have been abused are calling the Church. They may have convinced themselves that such change is not necessary, or that what is needed is some restorationist reform rather than an institutional metanoia. Yet, there can be no flight from the reality that now faces the Church. Those who think that they can restore the Church's dignity or that of its priests by dressing in ever more extravagant vestments, confusing liturgy with theater, thinking that God is somehow more attentive to a "sacred language" than to the unadorned prayer of the *anawim*, risk being the guardians of an empty tomb. They are deaf to the words of the angel: "Why do you seek the living among the dead?" They have forgotten the common dress and language of the God who comes *pro nobis*, transcendent in his very poverty and simplicity; whose dignity lies in the washing of our feet.

The Risen Christ is not the prisoner of history but its Lord and savior. A Church that confesses and follows him must understand that in order to be faithful to Christ in history, we must change ourselves in order to change history. This is the condition of the Church's very existence and mission: to witness more clearly and effectively to the Lord who alone can heal and restore what is human in a world that is desperately trying to remember what the human is.

The pope's letter is marking out the road we must take if we genuinely love the Church, the Body of Christ, and believe in her mission.

† LETTER TO THE PEOPLE OF GOD
August 20, 2018

"If one member suffers, all suffer together with it" (1 Cor 12:26). These words of Saint Paul forcefully echo in my heart as I acknowledge once more the suffering endured by many minors due to sexual abuse, the abuse of power, and the abuse of conscience perpetrated by a significant number of clerics and consecrated persons. These are crimes that inflict deep wounds of pain and powerlessness, primarily among the victims, but also among their family members and in the larger community of believers and nonbelievers alike. Looking back on the past, no effort to beg pardon and to seek to repair the harm done will ever be sufficient. Looking ahead to the future, no effort must be spared to create a culture that is able not only to prevent such situations from happening but also to prevent the possibility of their being covered up and perpetuated. The pain of the victims and their families is also our pain, and so it is urgent that we once more reaffirm our commitment to ensure the protection of minors and of vulnerable adults.

1. *If one member suffers...*

In recent days, a report was made public detailing the experiences of at least a thousand survivors, victims of sexual abuse, the abuse of power and of conscience at the hands of priests over a period of approximately seventy years. Even though it can be said that most of these cases belong to the past, nonetheless over time we have come to know the pain of many of the victims. We have realized that such wounds never disappear and that they require us to forcefully condemn these atrocities and join forces in uprooting this culture of death. These wounds never go away. The heart-wrenching pain of the victims, which cries out to heaven, was long ignored, kept quiet, or silenced. But their outcry was more powerful than all the measures meant to silence it, or sought to resolve it by oblique, complicit decisions that only intensified it. The Lord heard that cry and once again showed us on which side he stands. Mary's song is not mistaken, and its truth continues quietly to echo throughout history. For the Lord remembers the promise he made to our fathers: "He has scattered the proud in their conceit; he has cast down the mighty from their thrones and lifted up the lowly; he has filled the hungry with good things, and the rich he has sent away empty" (Lk 1:51–53). We feel shame when we realize that our style of life has contradicted, and continues to contradict, the words we recite.

With shame and repentance, we acknowledge as an ecclesial community that we were not where we should have been, that we did not act in a timely manner in realizing the magnitude and the gravity of the damage done to so many lives. We showed no care for the little ones; we abandoned them. I make my own the words of the then-Cardinal Ratzinger when, during the Way of the Cross composed for Good Friday 2005, he identified with the cry of pain of so many victims and exclaimed: "How much filth there is in the Church, and even among those who, in the priesthood, ought to belong entirely to [Christ]! How much pride, how much self-complacency! Christ's betrayal by his disciples, their unworthy reception of his body and blood, is certainly the greatest suffering endured by the Redeemer; it pierces his heart. We can only call to him from the depths of our hearts: *Kyrie eleison*— Lord, save us! (cf. Mt 8:25)" (Ninth Station).[1]

2. ...all suffer together with it

The extent and the gravity of all that has happened requires coming to grips with this reality in a comprehensive and communal way. While it is important and necessary on every journey of conversion to acknowledge the truth of what has happened, in itself this is not enough. Today we are challenged as the People of God to take on the pain of our brothers and sisters wounded in their flesh and in their spirit. If, in the past, the response was one of omission, today we need solidarity, in the deepest and most challenging sense, to become our way of forging present and future history. And we need to do this in an environment where conflicts, tensions, and above all the victims of every type of abuse can encounter an outstretched hand to protect them and rescue them from their pain (cf. *Evangelii Gaudium*, 228). Such solidarity demands that we in turn condemn whatever endangers the integrity of any person; it summons us to fight all forms of corruption, especially spiritual corruption. The latter is "a comfortable and self-satisfied form of blindness. Everything then appears acceptable: deception, slander, egotism and other subtle forms of self-centeredness, for 'even Satan disguises himself as an angel of light' (2 Cor 11:14)" (*Gaudate et Exsultate*, 165). Saint Paul's exhortation

---

1. http://www.vatican.va/news_services/liturgy/2005/via_crucis/en/station_09.html.

to suffer with those who suffer is the best antidote to all our attempts to repeat the words of Cain: "Am I my brother's keeper?" (Gen 4:9).

I am conscious of the effort and work being carried out in various parts of the world to come up with the necessary means to ensure the safety and protection of the integrity of children and of vulnerable adults, as well as implementing zero tolerance and ways of making all those who perpetrate or cover up these crimes accountable. We have delayed in applying these actions and sanctions that are so necessary, yet I am confident that they will help to guarantee a greater culture of care in the present and future.

Together with those efforts, every one of the baptized should feel involved in the ecclesial and social change that we so greatly need. This change calls for a personal and communal conversion to seeing things as the Lord does. For, as Saint John Paul II liked to say, "If we have truly started out anew from the contemplation of Christ, we must learn to see him especially in the faces of those with whom he wished to be identified" (*Novo Millenio Ineunte,* 49). To see things as the Lord does, to be where the Lord wants us to be, to experience a conversion of heart in his presence, prayer and penance will help. I invite the entire holy faithful People of God to a *penitential exercise of prayer and fasting*, following the Lord's command.[2] This can awaken our conscience and arouse our solidarity and commitment to a culture of care that says "never again" to every form of abuse.

It is impossible to think of a conversion of our activity as a Church that does not include the active participation of all the members of God's People. Indeed, whenever we have tried

---

2. "But this kind [of demon] does not come out except by prayer and fasting" (Mt 17:21).

to replace, or silence, or ignore, or reduce the People of God to small elites, we end up creating communities, projects, theological approaches, spiritualities and structures without roots, without memory, without faces, without bodies and ultimately, without lives.[3] This is clearly seen in a peculiar way of understanding the Church's authority, one common in many communities where sexual abuse and the abuse of power and conscience have occurred. Such is the case with clericalism, an approach that "not only nullifies the character of Christians, but also tends to diminish and undervalue the baptismal grace that the Holy Spirit has placed in the heart of our people."[4] Clericalism, whether fostered by priests themselves or by lay persons, leads to a segmentation in the ecclesial body that supports and helps to perpetuate many of the evils that we are condemning today. To say "no" to abuse is to say an emphatic "no" to all forms of clericalism.

It is always helpful to remember that "in salvation history, the Lord saved one people. We are never completely ourselves unless we belong to a people. That is why no one is saved alone as an isolated individual. Rather, God draws us to himself, taking into account the complex fabric of interpersonal relationships present in the human community. God wanted to enter into the life and history of a people" (*Gaudate et Exsultate*, 6). Consequently, the only way that we have for responding to this evil that has darkened so many lives is to experience it as a task that has to do with all of us as the People of God. This awareness of being part of a people and a shared history will enable us to acknowledge our past sins and mistakes with

---

3. Cf. "Letter to the Pilgrim People of God in Chile" (May 31, 2018).

4. Letter to Cardinal Marc Ouellet, President of the Pontifical Commission for Latin America (March 19, 2016).

a penitential openness that can allow us to be renewed from within. Without the active participation of all the Church's members, everything being done to uproot the culture of abuse in our communities will not be successful in generating the necessary dynamics for sound and realistic change. The penitential dimension of fasting and prayer will help us as God's People to come before the Lord and our wounded brothers and sisters as sinners imploring forgiveness and the grace of shame and conversion. In this way, we will find actions that can generate resources attuned to the Gospel. For "whenever we make the effort to return to the source and to recover the original freshness of the Gospel, new avenues arise, new paths of creativity open up, with different forms of expression, more eloquent signs and words with new meaning for today's world" (*Evangelii Gaudium*, 11).)

It is essential that we, as a Church, be able to acknowledge and condemn, with sorrow and shame, the atrocities perpetrated by consecrated persons, clerics, and all those entrusted with the mission of watching over and caring for those most vulnerable. Let us beg forgiveness for our own sins and the sins of others. An awareness of sin helps us to acknowledge the errors, the crimes, and the wounds caused in the past and allows us, in the present, to be more open and committed as we continue on a journey of renewed conversion.

Likewise, penance and prayer will help us to open our eyes and our hearts to other people's sufferings and to overcome the thirst for power and possessions that are so often the root of those evils. May fasting and prayer open our ears to the hushed pain felt by children, young people, and the disabled: a fasting that can make us hunger and thirst for justice and impel us to walk in the truth, supporting all the judicial measures that may be necessary; a fasting that shakes us up and leads us to be committed in truth and charity with all men and women of good will, and with society in general, to combatting all forms of the abuse of power, sexual abuse, and the abuse of conscience.

In this way, we can show clearly our calling to be "a sign and instrument of communion with God and of the unity of the entire human race" (*Lumen Gentium,* 1).

"If one member suffers, all suffer together with it," said Saint Paul. By an attitude of prayer and penance, we will become attuned as individuals and as a community to this exhortation, so that we may grow in the gift of compassion, in justice, prevention, and reparation. Mary chose to stand at the foot of her Son's cross. She did so unhesitatingly, standing firmly by Jesus' side. In this way, she revealed the way she lived her entire life. When we experience the desolation caused by these ecclesial wounds, we will do well, with Mary, "to insist more upon prayer," seeking to grow all the more in love and fidelity to the Church (St. Ignatius of Loyola, *Spiritual Exercises,* 319). She, the first of the disciples, teaches all of us as disciples how we are to stop before the sufferings of the innocent and take heed, without excuses or cowardice. To look to Mary is to discover the model of a true follower of Christ.

May the Holy Spirit grant us the grace of conversion and the interior anointing needed to express before these crimes of abuse our compunction and our resolve courageously to combat them.

Vatican City, 20 August 2018

Francis

PERMISSIONS

The following texts by Pope Francis are published with the permission of Libreria Editrice Vaticana: Letters to the Bishops of Chile (April 8, 2018; May 15 and 17, 2018); Letter to the Pilgrim People of God in Chile (May 31, 2018) and Letter to the People of God (August 20, 2018).

Thanks to *Ucanews.org* for permission to reprint the English translation of Jorge Mario Bergoglio's "The Doctrine of Tribulation" and the English translation of the essay by Fr. Diego Fares, "Against the Spirit of Fury." Thanks to *Thinking Faith*, the online journal of the Jesuits in Britain at www.thinkingfaith.org for reprinting the essay by Fr. James Hanvey, "Guide to Reading the 'Letter to the People of God.'" Thanks to Catholic News Agency (CNA) for the translation of Pope Francis's Letter to the Pilgrim People of God in Chile (May 31, 2018).

The Letters of the Superiors General of the Society of Jesus and all other Spanish and Italian texts were translated by Idea House (www.Ideahouse.biz). Special thanks to Celine Allen for additional work on the translations.

Scripture quotes are from the NRSV Edition, unless otherwise indicated.

www.ingramcontent.com/pod-product-compliance
Lightning Source LLC
Chambersburg PA
CBHW071004160426
43193CB00012B/1910